DIRA
BASIC
CHANNELING

ACCESSING DIVINE CONSCIOUSNESS

DIRA BASIC CHANNELING

ACCESSING DIVINE CONSCIOUSNESS

LUBNA KHARUSI

DIVINE • INTUITIVE • RECEPTIVE • AWARENESS
WWW.DIRAINTERNATIONAL.COM

DIRA BASIC CHANNELING
Accessing Divine Consciousness
Lubna Kharusi
Published by Dira Publishing Limited
85 Great Portland Street
London
W1W 7LT
United Kingdom

www.dirainternational.com

Copyright @ 2023 by Lubna Kharusi
All rights reserved.

No part of this publication may be reproduced, stored in a retrieval system, or transmitted in any form or by any means, electronic, mechanical, photocopying, recording or otherwise, without permission of the publisher.

Cover design by Lubna Kharusi

ISBN 978-1-912409-29-7

Any use of information in this book is at the reader's discretion and risk. Neither the author nor the publisher can be held responsible for any loss, claim, or damage arising out of the use, or misuse, of the contents contained herein.

www.dirainternational.com

TABLE OF CONTENTS

LETTER FROM LUBNA KHARUSI, FOUNDER OF DIRA 12

SET YOUR INTENTIONS 17

1. OVERVIEW 18
   1.1 The Dira Process of Learning How to Channel 20
      1.1.1 The Dira Induction 20
      1.1.2 The Dira Channeling Process 21
      1.1.3 Understanding Your Purpose on Earth 21
      1.1.4 Practice and Implementation: Learning How to Use and Apply Your Channel 22
      1.1.5 The Dira Level Program 23
   1.2 Terms & Overview of the Human Energetic System 24
   1.3 Dira Map for Chakra System 26

2. INTRODUCTION TO CHANNELING WITH DIRA 27
   2.1 Reflection 28
   2.2 What is Channeling? 29
   2.3 The History of Channeling and Modern-Day Consciousness. 29
   2.4 Dira Combines the Science of Hypnosis with Spirituality 32
   2.5 Scientific Study of Dira Channeling 34
   2.6 The Benefits of Channeling 37
   2.7 Understanding Channeling 40
      2.7.1 What is Channeling at Dira? 40
      2.7.2 What Do You Channel? 41
      2.7.3 How Do You Channel? 43

- 2.7.4 Summary on How Channeling Works 45
- 2.7.5 How can We Optimize Our 'Mind' with Channeling? 46
- 2.7.6 How Do You Experience Channel? 48
- 2.7.7 All Can Channel 49
- 2.7.8 Dira Map for Channeling Language & Expression 51
- 2.7.9 Reflection 52

2.8 Common Questions About Channeling 53
- 2.8.1 Do I need a Guru or objects to be able to channel The Divine? 53
- 2.8.2 Do I have to believe in God? 53
- 2.8.3 How long does it take to learn how to channel? 53
- 2.8.4 Does channeling contradict religion? 54
- 2.8.5 How is channeling different than prayer? 54
- 2.8.6 How can God speak through me? Isn't that only for special holy people? 54
- 2.8.7 Can you describe the channeling experience? 54
- 2.8.8 Will I be aware of what is happening? 55
- 2.8.9 How will I know that I am actually channeling The Divine? 55
- 2.8.10 Is channeling the same as meditation? 56

3. DIRA CHANNELING INDUCTION 57

3.1 The Process of Channel Induction 57
- 3.1.1 Dira Protocol for Dira Induction 63

3.2 Exercise: Dira Channeling Induction 65
- 3.2.1 Take a Break for Physical Exercise 78
- 3.2.2 Reflection 79

3.3 Why Can't I Visualize Anything in the Induction? 80
- 3.3.1 Dira Protocol for Muscle Test 83
- 3.3.2 Reflection 84

3.4 Do Things I See in the Induction Have Meaning? 85
- 3.4.1 I Saw Scary Things in the Induction 87
- 3.4.2 Reflection 88

3.5 I Have Forgotten My Keyword - Now What? 89

3.6 Falling Asleep During the Induction 89
   3.6.1 Reflection 91
3.7 Unable to Follow the Induction Instructions 92
   3.7.1 Reflection 94
3.8 Need More Help with The Induction 95

4. CHANNELING PROCESSES & GUIDELINES 96

4.1 Types of Channeling and When to Use Them 96
   4.1.2 The Golden Ball of Light 97
4.2 Requirements of Channeling 97
4.3 Pillar of White Light (Uses Induction Keyword) 99
4.4 Closing Your Channel 102
4.5 Dira Protocol for White Light Channeling 103
4.6 Questions About Channeling 105
   4.6.1 Are There Any Rituals to Channel? 105
   4.6.2 Channel in the Natural Way for Yourself 105
   4.6.3 When to Channel 106
   4.6.4 Can I Ask Channel About All Aspects of My Life? 108
   4.6.5 How Do I Know That I Am Safe When I Channel? 111
   4.6.6 What Determines the Clarity of Channel? 112
4.7 Physical Exercise Requirement When Channeling 114
4.8 Exercise: Dira Channeling Protocol AFTER Induction 117
   4.8.1 Reflection 121
4.9 How Do I Know I Am in Channel? 122
   4.9.1 Reflection 126
4.10 I Can't Focus and Stay in Channel 127
4.11 Ball of Golden Light Exercise & Explanation 128
   4.11.1 Dira Protocol for Ball of Golden Light Channeling 132
4.12 Physical Sensations & Symptoms in Channel 133

5. IMPROVE YOUR CHANNELING CAPABILITY 135

- 5.1 Help Dealing with Doubt 135
  - 5.1.1 Distinguishing Between Thoughts & Channel 137
  - 5.1.2 Comparing Your Channel to Other Channels 139
  - 5.1.3 Asking Others to Channel for You 140
- 5.2 Unblocking Your Channel 141
  - 5.2.1 Causes of Channeling Blocks 142
  - 5.2.2 Test if You Are Blocked 146
  - 5.2.3 Dira Protocol for Programming a Pendulum 148
- 5.3 Exercise: Difficulty Entering Channel 149
- 5.4 Improve Clarity of Channel 152
  - 5.4.1 Dira Protocol for The Dira Method 154
  - 5.4.2 Impact of Other Spiritual Practices on Channel 156
  - 5.4.3 The Need to Follow the Process 157
- 5.5 Measuring the Clarity of Channel 158
  - 5.5.1 Reflection 162
- 5.6 Channeling with a Partner 163
  - 5.6.1 Process of Channeling with a Partner 163

6. HELP WITH UNDERSTANDING THE MESSAGES FROM CHANNEL 168

- 6.1 Where Does the Light Come From? 168
- 6.2 What Do the Images I See Mean? 169
  - 6.2.1 Dira Protocol for Understanding Channeled Messages & Imagery 171
- 6.3 The Timeline of Channel Vs Physical Timing 172
- 6.4 I Get Different Answers to the Same Question 173
- 6.5 Why Would People Channel Different Answers? 174

7. MOVING FORWARD 176
7.1 Seek Divine Perspective 176
7.2 Teaching Channeling to Others 177
7.3 How to Use Channeling to Change Your Life 179
7.3.1 Calling on Divine Properties 179
7.3.2 Dira Protocol for Calling on Divine Properties 180
7.4 Conclusion 181
7.4.1 Summary of our suggested next steps: 183

8. ABOUT THE AUTHOR 185
8.1 Books by Lubna Kharusi 186

This book is a companion guide to Dira's Basic Channeling Program.

To purchase the program, scan the QR code below.

DIRA BASIC CHANNELING PROGRAM

A dedication to:

Let's light up this world together.

With gratitude,

LETTER FROM LUBNA KHARUSI, FOUNDER OF DIRA

This book contains one of the most powerful techniques of human awakening that exists and has been 'downloaded' from Source itself to enable the shift of collective consciousness from separation to Oneness. The Dira Method enables a conscious connection to Source Energy.

The Dira Method not only has completely changed my own life but also the lives of many all over the world who have experienced Dira, as Dira and its unfolding is a Divine plan. It doesn't come from the mind of an individual such as myself, it is a catalyst for the shift of human consciousness and the transition from the realm of physicality (or 3D as some name it) to a realm of Oneness.

Separation is the torment of our existence. It is in separation that we experience pain, suffering, lack, and illness, just to remind us, and call us back to the conscious awareness that we have the capacity as humans to shift our perspective of witnessing and embodiment to that of Oneness (Divine's perspective). The by-product of this shift into alignment with Divinity is physical, emotional, mental, spiritual, and life healing.

So, what is needed to experience this other than being human? Belief. Belief in a consciousness greater than our individualized consciousness, and perhaps even greater than all collective consciousness, the Omnipotent, Omniscient, Omnipresent consciousness of the creator of this realm and that which we have incarnated in our bodies to witness as One. This Source of all interpermeates everything in existence, including us, and this realm of separation was created for it to be witnessed through our uniquely diverse perspectives.

Dira is not limited by religion and holds a perspective that recognizes the Oneness of truth in all religions. In all religious and esoteric paths, there is a common theme of the coming to conscious awareness of Source Energy, and although different names are used such as God, Allah, Yahweh, and Par Brahman, all religions offer a gateway to the conscious awareness of the same Divine Source Energy.

I do not take credit or blame for what you experience from this book, Dira, and your journey, it is all a Divine plan, and each is responsible for their own journey. This book contains philosophy, techniques, and vibrations, and it is all channeled, as are all offerings by Dira. However, it is not random that this book has arrived in your experience, it comes as a gift, a call, and an answer to your inner longing.

The vision of Dira is to make a global shift for humanity from separation to Oneness by teaching people how to connect to Divine Source directly. Collective consciousness is currently at a level of understanding that we are separate from one another, living in a realm of duality, because our physical senses provide information that reinforces that belief. For example, we think we end at our skin, but our energy field radiates out far beyond the skin. We can touch, see, hear, smell, and taste things that are perceived to be outside of us, separate from us, and associate our identity with a physical body, a personality, or events of our lives.

As humans we can look at the world through many windows, one may be that we are physical beings for which we use our physical senses, another may be that we are energetic frequencies of vibration where we can use our intangible senses, like our 'sixth sense'; and another may be that we are One with everything connected in Divine Source Energy. One can use the term they feel comfortable with, but for us at Dira, Divine Source refers to the Ultimate Energy of Everything.

This conscious perspective and experience of vibrational energy and Oneness is the focus of Dira's philosophy, but instead of philosophizing about it too much, we provide tools for people to open their capacity to experience it directly, as experience cannot be denied, and is within the reach of everyone. Just because someone has not yet experienced the conscious perspective of Oneness, or that we are energetically connected, doesn't mean it is not possible or that it is not a natural part of the human's capacity for conscious awareness. In the same way, if someone keeps their eyes closed, it doesn't mean that they can't see, they just choose to keep their eyes closed, because they have been conditioned to do so, but their sense of sight exists, they are just not using that capacity.

At Dira, we enable people who want to experience and embody an expanded human experience by becoming a channel of Divine Source Energy, where one can come to understand the expansiveness of what they are and how they are connected to everything in existence.

DIRA is an acronym for our method to enable this process; Divine-Intuitive-Receptive-Awareness.

We believe that being a channel of Source Energy is an integral part of human capacity. Unfortunately, through conditioning and mental constructs, we have prevented ourselves from accessing this natural state of connection, limiting ourselves, because of the reinforced beliefs of socio-historical constructs of what people interpret and believe to be possible.

And what is the point of being able to channel Divine? To enable people to live the most magnificent possibility if they want to. Channeling Source affects all aspects of life, as it shifts the level of consciousness from which you function. You can consider consciousness to be the state of awareness from which you operate. For example, if you make a decision using logic, where consciousness is in the mental body, logic is limited to deriving conclusions based on historical data collection. However, Source consciousness has no limitation of information as it holds all that ever was, is, or will be - it is Omniscient, and in Oneness there is no time or space, so all is. Therefore, if someone has the option to use the mental body or Source, which would you choose, the one that has limited information or the one that holds all information? We provide you with a method to access Divine Source.

At Dira we believe that this will be the way that people will live all over the world. In the same way that people all over the world use the internet, people all over the world will channel Divine Source Energy, it is just a matter of time.

"Channeling is part of the
human capacity –
as Source is always
communicating –
the question is,
are you listening?"

 **SET YOUR INTENTIONS**

Take a few moments to write down your intentions.

By writing your intentions, you focus the energy.

Although this book is already documented, the energy that you experience is LIVE as you go through it, and 98% of what you experience during reading and practicing is energetic.

Make some notes about the following:
1. What brought you to want to read this book and follow this program?
2. What do you hope to get out of it?
3. What do you intend for yourself by learning how to channel Divine?
4. How would you like it to help you shift your life?
5. Are you open to experiencing Divine Source Energy?

1. OVERVIEW

Welcome to the Dira Basic Channeling method, where you will learn how to connect with Divine Source Energy through enabling an experience of Divine.

For your reference and convenience, the Basic Channeling Program is available on the Dira online platform, www.dirainternational.com, or scan the following QR code.

DIRA BASIC CHANNELING PROGRAM

NOTE: This book is intended as a companion guide to the Dira Basic Channeling Program. Channeling is a vibrational experience, and reading the transcript of the program is not equivalent to listening to and experiencing it.

Dira International is an organization that teaches people how to channel and offers channeled programs and retreats for people to experience and realize their truth and potential by channeling Divine Source Energy. The vision of Dira is to make a global shift for humanity from separation to Oneness, resulting in the transmutation of the vibration of the world and cosmos.

To find out more about Dira's programs and how you can learn to be a channel visit www.dirainternational.com or scan the following QR code.

WWW.DIRAINTERNATIONAL.COM

This book is considered a companion guide to all of the Dira programs and the Dira Level Retreats, as every program and retreat of Dira is done in channel. The source material for this book includes transcripts from the Basic Channeling Programs conducted at Casa Dira between 2017 and 2023 that were channeled through Lubna Kharusi. We apologize for the inconvenience if the language style is not the way you would expect a book to be written.

The text contained from chapter three onwards is channeled material. It is the words and perspective of Divine. Unless stated otherwise. Furthermore, text in *italics* is not channeled material.

Divine Source refers to itself in the channeled sessions as the collective: 'We, Us, Our'.

In order not to name the individuals who asked the questions, they will be referred to as 'Participant'.

The information provided in this book is for general informational purposes only. The information is not intended to be a substitute for professional health or medical advice or treatment, nor should it be relied upon for the diagnosis, prevention, or treatment of any health consideration. Consult with a licensed health care practitioner before altering or discontinuing any medications, treatment, or care, or starting any diet, exercise, or supplementation program.

Dira information, programs and content (including this book) are for the facilitation of an experience of spiritual alignment with the soul and Divine light. They are not a replacement for any other form of therapy, medical intervention, or religion, and are only complementary. The by-product of alignment with Divinity through an experience, might enable release, however, we always recommend that one should address any discomfort, be it internal or external, at all levels of their being, including physically, emotionally, mentally, energetically, and spiritually.

1.1 THE DIRA PROCESS OF LEARNING HOW TO CHANNEL

1.1.1 THE DIRA INDUCTION

The Dira Induction uses a method of hypnosis to guide the participant into a deep state of trance channel, where they are consciously aware, but their thoughts and emotions are 'parked to the side' so that the experience of Divine vibration becomes dominant. The Induction provides the EXPERIENCE of Divine.

In the Induction, the participant is encouraged to place a 'keyword'. This keyword establishes the neural pathway that can then bring them back into the experience whenever they like and enter into a state of channel. The more one channels using this keyword, the more established the neural pathway.

The Dira Induction is part of the **Dira Basic Channeling Program**, which is the content of this book. It should be noted that the Induction is a vibrational experience and in the Dira Basic Channeling Program the Induction is a sound file. Although the transcript of the Induction is included in this book, reading it is not the same as experiencing it with the recording.

You can purchase the Dira Basic Channeling program below:

DIRA BASIC CHANNELING PROGRAM

1.1.2 THE DIRA CHANNELING PROCESS

The Dira Channeling Process is the technique for entering into channel on your own following the Induction. It is also a form of self-hypnosis, where you use the neural pathway from the keyword established in the Induction, to be able to enter channel quickly, on command, and in your control. The Dira Channeling Process is taught in the **Dira Basic Channeling Program,** which is the content of this book.

1.1.3 UNDERSTANDING YOUR PURPOSE ON EARTH

The **Magnificent Possibility** book explains the perspective of channel for the key questions about life. What are you? Why are you here? What is Divine? The toolkits humans have been provided with to fulfill their purpose on earth etc. This book also provides an important foundational understanding of your human and soul experience. Everybody should read this book, whether or not they choose to channel, as it brings a clear understanding of the purpose of existence. You can scan the following QR code to purchase the book.

THE MAGNIFICENT POSSIBILITY

1.1.4 PRACTICE AND IMPLEMENTATION: LEARNING HOW TO USE AND APPLY YOUR CHANNEL

Once you have learned how to channel, Dira offers many protocols and techniques of how to use channel to help you in your life. These protocols are taught and explained in the **Dira Advanced Channeling Program** and book. The Dira Advanced Channeling Program offers over 30 Dira protocols and exercises for how to use channeling in your life so that you can experience the benefits of channel. The program is in video format and includes reference charts and protocol summary sheets. The book is the transcript of the program. As the program is channeled, the exercises offer a vibrational experience that cannot be experienced in the same way by just reading the book. The book is meant to be a reference guide for those completing the Online Program. You can scan the QR codes next.

DIRA ADVANCED CHANNELING PROGRAM

DIRA ADVANCED CHANNELING BOOK

1.1.5 THE DIRA LEVEL PROGRAM

The **Dira Level Program** takes you on a journey through seven levels to embody your Divinity over approximately three years, depending on how long the individual chooses to take. The Level Program uses **The Dira Method**, a comprehensive practice for coming to embody your light as a human being. The first two Levels are live group retreats, and Levels 3-7 are done at your own pace individually, with support.

The Level Program provides the guidance, practice, and tools to embody your light and fulfill your soul's purpose on earth. Change comes through practice, knowledge, experience, and embodiment, and the Level Program provides the infrastructure for you to live your most magnificent possibility!

DIRA LEVEL PROGRAM

1.2 TERMS & OVERVIEW OF THE HUMAN ENERGETIC SYSTEM

The following terms will be used throughout this book and Dira's contents overall, and therefore it is important that you familiarize yourself with them.

Aura: The total energy field of a human or living being, and it radiates out beyond your physical body.

The Chakra System: is the energetic system of the body. You can look at it like a factory, and each chakra is a machine in the factory that processes a color spectrum of energy.

Chakra: The energetic centers in the energy system of the body that process different color spectra of energy.

Crown Chakra: Located at the top of the head and is the interface to white light (Divine energy).

Heart Chakra: Located in the center of the chest and is the portal interface for Divine love (golden light).

Divine: Source Energy, God, Collective Consciousness, Allah, Elohim, Yahweh, Par Brahman, Supreme Being, The Creator of all, Omnipotent, Omniscient, Omnipresent Source of Everything.

Transmutation: Shifting from one vibration to a higher vibration.

Vibration: Energy frequency.

The following chart provides an overview of the energetic system that will be referred to in this program. From the chart and diagram, you are able to see the location of each chakra in your body, the color of the light that it processes, the energy body that it relates to, and the element that is used in The Dira Method for cleansing and energizing.

If you would like to learn more about your energetic system, chakras, and how they relate to your life, please refer to The Magnificent Possibility book.

THE MAGNIFICENT POSSIBILITY

DIRA MAP FOR CHAKRA SYSTEM

Reference Chart RC 001

CHAKRA	POSITION	COLOR	ENERGY BODY	ELEMENT
CROWN CHAKRA		VIOLET	DIVINE	WHITE LIGHT
AJNA OR 3RD EYE		INDIGO	SOUL	REFRACTED COLORED LIGHT
THROAT CHAKRA		BLUE	MENTAL BODY	SOUND
HEART CHAKRA		GREEN	ASTRAL BODY	AIR
SOLAR PLEXUS		YELLOW	EGOIC BODY	FIRE
SEX/ SACRAL CHAKRA		ORANGE	EMOTIONAL BODY	WATER
ROOT CHAKRA		RED	PHYSICAL BODY	EARTH

2. INTRODUCTION TO CHANNELING WITH DIRA

This section delves into the process of channeling, which involves tapping into our intuition and accessing the Omniscient field of information. This field contains knowledge of the past, present, and future, allowing us to make decisions based on a broader perspective than just our logical minds.

Take a few moments to reflect on this possibility using the reflection sheet on the following page. The possibility that you have this capacity to experience Divine.

 **REFLECTION**

Take a moment to reflect on the questions below:

1. In what ways have I silenced my inner voice?
2. How was Divine communicating with me all along?

2.2 WHAT IS CHANNELING?

One could say that we have all been channeling all our lives, but we tend to ignore it, as we all have intuition, insight, and inspiration, which is Divine communication through us.

Intuition is a part of human capacity and experience, but we have conditioned ourselves to turn down that voice inside us that wants to be expressed, by choosing logic and societal conditioning to take precedence.

At Dira, we teach simple techniques of how to use self-hypnosis to turn down the dominance of the conscious mind and mental chatter, so that the voice of intuition and inspiration is clear and can be accessed on demand. We refer to this as channeling.

With the Dira channeling method, the guidance that then flows through you is that of The Divine Source. The Divine is a term used to refer to the Ultimate Source of Everything. Some say 'God', others perhaps 'Universal Consciousness'; there are many such terms, and you may use the word that resonates best for you that refers to Ultimate Source Energy.

2.3 THE HISTORY OF CHANNELING AND MODERN-DAY CONSCIOUSNESS

Genius, or the ones who were exceptionally creative - have always accessed their creation from the field of Divine or an expanded consciousness. The word genius originated from the notion that one was connected to spirit; it is different than intelligence - genius is considered bestowed upon people. The genius offered could be art, music, innovation, literature, or even sportsmanship. And famous geniuses like Tesla, Chopin, Mozart, Michael Jackson, Shakespeare, Einstein, Tiger Woods, and others, all communicated that they entered a trance-like state to access their 'Genius' - they entered into an altered state of consciousness. Sometimes those moments of genius occurred randomly - a moment of inspiration, or they may even have used substances to bring on those states.

Throughout history, those who were channels of Divine also became religious guides, at least those whose 'Genius' message related to the message of Divine for humanity at the time. Sharing what they channeled of Divine in religion or spiritual guidance, and they were considered 'enlightened' beings.

Whether a genius or a prophet, it was considered that being able to channel Source was reserved for only a special few, as they either experienced it spontaneously or randomly or were considered 'chosen'. However, religion and spiritual practices always provided the path and guidance of how all could reach an experience of Divine bliss - that if people followed the practices and guidance of the one who could channel, they could potentially one day experience Divine bliss as well (if not in this life, then in the afterlife).

Aside from religion, there was also the other possibility, which was to use psychotropic drugs, DMT, plant medicine, dance, drums, or other practices, which also induced trance-like states, where more people had access to this field of expanded consciousness but were unable to control or manage the forces of energy that they channeled. These practices tended to be restricted to the spiritual leaders, medicine men, or shamans, to protect the masses from possible harm and not being able to handle the potential dangers of these experiences that were not controlled.

The collective is now entering a golden age, where consciousness is yearning to elevate. Human beings have always been seeking the experience of Divine because this is why we have been created, to experience and witness Divinity. More and more people are seeking to fill the void within them and return to this experience of union with Divine, as they realize that the materiality of life doesn't fill the void within - that void can only be filled with Divine light.

So, people turn to tools outside of them like the popularization of plant medicine, psychotropic drugs, and various practices in a desperate seeking of this Divine experience, as the messages of most religions have become so distorted over time, that people no longer resonate with what is currently being presented due to the politicization and power struggles of religion.

But what if you were told that you can access Divine just because you are human and that this is your birthright? That you don't need to be special, good enough, or 'chosen'. And that you don't need to use something outside of you like drugs or plant medicine to induce a trance. And that you can experience Divine consciousness anytime you want and be sure that the energy that you are accessing is Divine.

It is time for humanity to know and experience Divinity without an intermediary, but through their direct experience, as then that knowing of Divine cannot be unknown, as once you know it, you can't dismiss it. And as Divine becomes known through direct experiences of the collective, the consciousness of earth will elevate.

How does this happen? By combining spirituality with proven scientific methods. Science wasn't as advanced as 1400, 2000, or 4000 years ago. Hence, not everyone could channel - it only happened randomly with prophets or gurus or was controlled by shamans. But now, through the evolution and discoveries of mind sciences, the possibility for everyone to be able to channel has presented itself.

In the same way that science has enabled progress in communications through the development of the internet - something that was perceived as impossible in the past, that a human being could have access to such a vast amount of data, information, and connectivity with every human on earth - now through mind sciences, we can be connected to Divine collective consciousness as well.

2.4 DIRA COMBINES THE SCIENCE OF HYPNOSIS WITH SPIRITUALITY

At Dira, we combine the science of self-hypnosis with spirituality, to be able to enter trance states on demand and fully in control. Clinical research over the last half-century has provided robust evidence of the power of hypnosis in psychotherapy for dealing with PTSD, pain management, addiction release, etc. But what if we took it even further? What if we integrated hypnosis with spiritual practice? Imagine how profound the impact and experience would be! And this is what Dira has done.

The goal of all spiritual practice is to come to know and experience Divine Source Energy. Hypnosis enables an openness to new experiences and suggestibility. By using hypnotic Inductions, the conscious brain becomes overstimulated, and the barrier to the subconscious mind opens, resulting in a hypnotic state or trance state.

If we are to consider that by using self-hypnosis, one can achieve this state in a controlled manner in just a few minutes. Through hypnosis, you can experience and achieve trance experiences that are the goal of most spiritual practices without the need for rituals, drugs, or years of spiritual practice - or being 'chosen by God'. Hypnosis provides the possibility for EVERYONE willing to self-hypnotize themselves to have this capability to enter a trance and experience Divine, if they want to.

Through brain imaging, scientists have discovered that hypnosis works by calming down parts of the brain activity such as the capacity to switch between thoughts and tasks, self-awareness, as well as automatic functions like heart rate, breathing, and blood flow, bringing the participant into deep relaxation.

Once someone is in a trance, they become open to suggestions and possibilities, because the mental chatter is parked. So all of the beliefs and conditioning about not being worthy of Divine are also set to the side, and there is this wonderful opportunity that you can make use of this trance state to access something that is the reason why you have been born, the reason why there is always a sense of feeling empty or unsatisfied, as Divine consciousness has always been calling you to witness it and be conscious of its presence within you.

The Dira Method of channeling uses the openness of the mind from hypnotic trance states and guides people into profound spiritual experiences of Divine. At Dira each person is empowered to access Divine consciousness in a controlled manner, without an intermediary or the use of anything outside of you.

2.5 SCIENTIFIC STUDY OF DIRA CHANNELING

So how do you confirm that channeling works? How do you prove something nonphysical with science, when science, by definition, is about proving things in the physical world? So, at Dira we have decided that the best way to demonstrate scientifically the effectiveness of channeling, and that something actually happens, is to measure the physical state of the body.

And we did a study on brain activity, and how the brain pulsation and brain frequencies change from channel to non-channel state. So, the Institute of Noetic Sciences Discovery Lab (IONS) in California collected measures during Dira channeling states and normal mind-wandering states and analyzed the data for any differences between the two conditions in a study that was approved by the Institute of Noetic Sciences Institutional Review Board.

Comparing Dira channeling and mind-wandering states, the average scores of participants show evidence that demonstrates that the brain waves, generalized across the brain, are different in channel using The Dira Method compared to that of a non-channel mind-wandering state.

Using The Dira Method, we were able to demonstrate that indeed there was a shift in brain activity. What was interesting to note is that in this study, it was seen that the entire brain was affected across all wavelengths, so in the Delta, Theta, Alpha, Beta, and Gamma wavelengths. Furthermore, usually, in these studies on meditation with monks, it is shown predominantly in the prefrontal cortex that the Theta waves are affected, but with Dira channeling, it was shown that the whole brain was affected, across all wavelengths.

This in itself doesn't demonstrate that channeling works, but it certainly demonstrates that something happens inside, that is different from your normal mind wandering state. Furthermore, at the time of the study, which was in 2019, this was the first study that IONS had participated in that demonstrated that channeling actually causes a biological response. They had done a channeling study in the past, where there was no clear evidence of a shift in brainwaves. However, with The Dira Method we were able to demonstrate that indeed there was a shift in brain activity.

The image on the following page shows the brain activity of Dira participants in channel versus normal mind-wandering state This image is provided by IONs.

Following this study, Dira was referenced in the book The Science of Channeling, by Helané Wahbeh, as a method that scientifically has shown evidence that channeling is possible and causes a shift in brain activity. Moving forward, we intend to increase the sample size as more and more people start to channel. And to be able to tell across the different levels of Dira, how great an impact there is on the brain waves, as it is assumed that the further you move along in your Level Program, the greater the impact on your brain waves.

We have also seen that pupil dilation is impacted, heart rate is impacted, breath is impacted, as well as other biological functions. Studies like this will take years to conclude, but the beginning has started, and right from the beginning, it was clear something in the body happens when you enter into channel.

	CHANNEL	**NORMAL**
DELTA **(0.5-4 Hz)**	Spectrum - EO, Divine silent, 0.5-4Hz	Spectrum - EO, Mind-Wandering, 0.5-4Hz 61.8 / 57 / 52.2 / 47.5 / 42.7
THETA **(4-8 Hz)**	Spectrum - EO, Divine silent, 4-8Hz	Spectrum - EO, Mind-Wandering, 4-8Hz 54.1 / 50.4 / 46.7 / 43 / 39.4
ALPHA **(8-13 Hz)**	Spectrum - EO, Divine silent, 8-13Hz	Spectrum - EO, Mind-Wandering, 8-13Hz 58.4 / 53.8 / 49.3 / 44.8 / 40.3
BETA **(12-32 Hz)**	Spectrum - EO, Divine silent, 12-32Hz	Spectrum - EO, Mind-Wandering, 12-32Hz 48.4 / 45.6 / 42.7 / 39.8 / 36.9
GAMMA **(32-50 Hz** **or higher)**	Spectrum - EO, Divine silent, 32-55Hz	Spectrum - EO, Mind-Wandering, 32-55Hz 46.9 / 41.8 / 36.8 / 31.7 / 26.7

2.6 THE BENEFITS OF CHANNELING

The benefits of channeling are vast. Imagine that there is a pool of data that has information about everything that has ever happened. Imagine if you could access this pool directly. What can this mean for us?

To start, imagine if you could access all of the information presented to you since you were conceived; every sound you heard, every sensation you felt, every flavor you tasted, every sight you saw, every experience you lived, all right there for you to access, without the corruption of biases or limiting beliefs attached to any of it. What would you be able to do with such an ability? Or rather, what would you not be able to do?

Channeling enables the possibility of widening this opening to be able to retrieve more information and hold a wider perspective than logic can. Not only are you able to access all the data in your own subconscious mind, but you are also able to plug into the Universal Mind for everything as it is Omniscient, and that is where the vastness of this ability blossoms.

By channeling, you are not limited by logic, which is based on historical data collection and conclusions derived from historical experiences, but instead, you access information and conclusions based on an infinite data pool, guided by The Omniscient Divine; a data pool that is detached from, and not corrupted by, your mental constructs, societal beliefs, and other irrelevant factors. On a practical level, by channeling, you are able to access information that will help you make decisions in life that are more aligned for you, and so in turn, serve you versus not. Decisions that will allow you to live your most Magnificent Possibility. Want to know how best to write your resume? Channel. Want to compose a piece of music? Channel. Want to understand how to handle a conflict with someone? Channel. The list is endless, as this is an inherent human ability we are all born with and meant to use anytime we wish.

The goal of Dira is to offer a result of transmutation, and therefore it was critical for us to be able to measure the changes that participants experienced in their lives.

We conducted a qualitative analysis of the effects of Channeling with Dira on the lives of participants through surveys and feedback submissions. Below is a summary of the collection of data up to March of 2024, and includes feedback from Basic Channelers all the way to participants who have completed their Level 7.

The results on the following page show the percentage of participants that experienced the listed changes in their lives.

Benefits of Channeling with Dira	% +ve Response
Mental wellbeing	100%
Emotional wellbeing	100%
Spiritual wellbeing	100%
Connection to Divine & faith	100%
Shifting perspective	96%
Learning new information	96%
Finding purpose	96%
Gaining clarity	92%
Manifesting a better life	92%
Improving relationships	92%
Resolving personal issues	88%
Finding inner peace	88%
Trusting your intuition	88%
Receiving inspiration	88%
Interacting beyond the veil of separation	88%
Coming out from hiding your light	83%
Community, friends & belonging	79%
Financial growth & abundance	79%
Better decision making	79%
Physical healing of ailments	75%
Letting go of masks you used to wear	75%
Increasing sixth senses & related capabilities	75%
Physical wellbeing	75%
Overcoming unhealthy habits	63%
Increased creativity	63%

2.7 UNDERSTANDING CHANNELING

Just to give a little background about channeling at Dira. So, channeling is a way to park your mental thoughts and emotions on the side and allow a connection with Divine Source Energy. So, we're always connected to Divine in our lives, and it comes about in the form of intuition or insight. And so, when we have a gut feeling, or we have an inner knowing, this is basically Divine speaking to us and guiding us.

But what tends to happen is that with our mental thoughts, we tend to override that feeling and say, 'No my logic knows more'. So channeling is a way to do the opposite. It's a way to park your logic and your mental thoughts, and you allow this intuition to become amplified and clear. And so, you are allowing the Divine aspect of yourself to be known, heard, witnessed, experienced. The objective at the end of the day is to have an understanding, from a broad perspective, of your connection with Divine. And for you to be able to channel yourselves.

And so channeling also, just as a note, is a part of the human capacity. Everyone can do it, in the same way, that everyone has intuition, everyone can channel. So, it's not that it's something that you need to practice for many years, or you need to be on a certain path, or a certain belief system. If you believe that there is an Ultimate Source of Everything and that you can connect to it, and you are within it, then you can channel.

2.7.1 WHAT IS CHANNELING AT DIRA?

Channeling is the enablement of Divine Source Energy to speak through you, to be experienced by you, and to be expressed through your being. So, it is the subsiding of mental thoughts, ego, and emotions, so that Divine Source Energy flows through you.

It also is most appropriate for your soul's composition. Meaning that, in the purpose of your existence, your channel will have its utmost clarity and appropriateness for the fulfillment of your purpose, which is to witness your own Divinity, and for the witnessing of that Divinity to be compounded by the witnessing of others of your Divinity.

In channel you have this infinite library. When you are channeling Divine Source Energy, you imagine the library is white light, and there are an infinite number of books in it. And then the Divine, Ultimate Supreme Consciousness, will offer which book is appropriate for you. This is how channeling is practiced at Dira.

In other places, perhaps, they channel specific books, so for example, someone says I have my angels, I have my guide, I have my jinn (entities), I have my ancestor, whatever it is that they are specifically channeling, is one book in the library, and it is limiting, and there's no need to limit yourself. So here at Dira, you learn how to channel Omniscient, Divine Source Energy, and then the Omniscient provides what is most appropriate for you.

2.7.2 WHAT DO YOU CHANNEL?

So, what are you channeling? What is being spoken through you? What do you sense when you sense physical sensation when you enter into channel? What do you see? It is Divine communication. Everyone has their own unique way of channeling. What is consistent is perspective. So, from channeled space it is a wide perspective, it is not a conditioned perspective. Furthermore, from channeled space, there is no emotion. So, it is unbiased and impartial.

And so, if you were to imagine, that you are each refracted spectrum of Divine light, the channel that you are allowing to be witnessed and experienced through you, is the amplified unlimited version of your spectrum of vibration. In addition, because it is between the crown and the heart, the crown allows white light to flow through you, and so whatever relevant aspects of white light that also need to be experienced through you, will be. So, it is not that it is just your soul you are channeling. You are channeling Divine Omnipresent, Omniscient, Omnipotent white light, through a funnel of spectrum of vibration.

So, normally when you interact in your day-to-day life, it is through the funnel of the conscious mind. So, it is narrowing it down even more. When people refer to talking to their higher soul, then it is just their refracted light. In Divine channel, it is white light, but there is perspective and appropriateness for your spectrum of vibration. So, what does that mean in terms of appropriate? So, for example, if someone's spectrum of vibration is in blue, you can say that they are creative and expressive, then they would be able to channel things like art, as an example.

Someone else may have a different spectrum of vibration, and then they are able to, for example, if it's to do with physical implementation, then perhaps they are able to channel detailed formulas for the creation of a physical machine, as an example. So, each one, what they are able to channel, in its magnificent form, is related to their spectrum of vibration, and why they are on this earth.

So, if you see someone who can channel physics formula, and you are unable to channel physics formula, it is not that your channel is blocked, it is that the channel is appropriate for each refraction of spectrum of vibration, so it's for your purpose on this earth. But all come from Divine. So, whether or not you compose symphonies, or you create and come to a medical breakthrough, the Source is the same, Divine white light.

2.7.3 HOW DO YOU CHANNEL?

And so, how is this achieved? Or the state of trance achieved? It is through a standard method of self-hypnosis. And so, in hypnosis, you move from the conscious mind into the subconscious mind, typically. For the purpose of channeling, you move then from the subconscious mind, to what you can call the Universal Mind or Divine Source.

So, the Universal Mind is that which is the collection of all data, not just your own specific data. The subconscious mind would be the collection of your own specific data. So, it's taken a step further, where you don't only move to the subconscious, you also move beyond to the Universal Mind. And then in the state of channel, you can access that which is Omniscient presence, it is the Divine aspect and connection to you.

So, from the logical perspective, if you were to know, that you collect all of this data on your hard drive - thousands and thousands, millions and millions of stimuli registered in the mind.

And then you have the software, which starts to retrieve this data, which are your beliefs and perceptions. So, this software not only retrieves the data from your own mind, but it also becomes the script for your experience, because you are connected and One with everything. And so, whatever goes on in your head also goes on in your life experience, it is just mirrored to you.

And so, you have the software, and sometimes the software has viruses, that create uncomfortable scenarios. So, the virus may be, 'I'm not enough', or 'love is conditional', as an example. And then, the data you retrieve from your mind reinforces this belief that you're not enough. So, for example, the math teacher tells you, 'You're bad at math', and then you are unable to do math problems because you keep on reinforcing to yourself that you're bad at math. There is also the scenario outside of you, that reflects that you're bad at math, and so, for example, the test that comes up is very difficult, etc.

Your experience of life becomes the mirror of your thoughts. And so, the software of the mind, when it is not aligned with the soul's knowing, creates discomfort.

But so, what happens in logic? Logic is the interpretation of historical data. And therefore, there is the deduction of conclusions in some way. But they are based on a limited perspective. So, from the conscious mind level, you may have a 10-degree or 15-degree opening of the information available. Whereas from the space of intuition, there is no filter based on beliefs, because the beliefs reflect that which is infinite.

So, if the belief is 'Love is infinite', then there is no filter in what data can be retrieved. And so, this infinite belief, or the belief of the soul's knowing, becomes an Omniscient field, or frame of reference that has all information. And in this Omniscient frame of reference, because it is in the vibration of Oneness, or the space of Oneness, it also knows all information, not only of the past but also the present and the future. Because in the space of Oneness, there is no time, and so everything exists simultaneously.

So, your intuition has the knowing also of everything that is to come, not only about the past. Whereas logic will make patterns of what could potentially reoccur based on historical conclusions, it doesn't mean that your future will be a repetition of your past. And in the space of intuition, in the space of Oneness, it is not dependent on the past, it knows everything.

2.7.4 SUMMARY ON HOW CHANNELING WORKS

The Components of the Human Mind:

Our Hard drive (The Subconscious Mind): In every minute of our lives, we receive at least 4000 message units of data that are stored in the mind from the time that we were in the womb. This data is stored in our subconscious mind, like the hard drive of a computer.

The Internet (The Universal Mind): Furthermore, there is an electromagnetic field that radiates out of us that connects all hard drives like a network, connecting the subconscious minds of all, into what can be referred to as a Universal Mind, you can consider it like the internet.

RAM (The Conscious Mind): The data that we retrieve from the hard drive, or our subconscious mind, lies in the conscious mind, like our RAM. At any point in time, the conscious mind only uses 10% to 12% of all the data stored on the hard drive.

The Software (Beliefs & Perceptions): So, if all of this data is available, the question is how do we retrieve it by the conscious mind? The retrieval mechanism is the software of the mind, which for humans are our beliefs and perceptions. Our beliefs are like the word search, we only retrieve what is searched for, and our search is based on a programmed software.

Viruses (Limiting Beliefs): When we hold limiting beliefs, we can consider them like a virus that corrupts our software to retrieve and access data. So, for example, if one believes that they are bad at math, the software will retrieve data that reinforces that belief, and so then indeed they become bad at math. But if for example, they had a different belief, such as math is easy, then the data retrieved based on this software program would reflect that.

2.7.5 HOW CAN WE OPTIMIZE OUR 'MIND' WITH CHANNELING?

Channeling is a process of releasing limiting beliefs so that the conscious mind can access more data that is relevant to us, opening the window from the conscious mind to the subconscious and Universal Mind. It is the removal of viruses in our software that limit us and our potential.

As societies, we have been conditioned to believe (a programmed belief) that our logical reasoning at the conscious mind level is superior to intuition. When the conscious mind, as has been explained, is limited to a small window of data based on historical data collection and conditioned beliefs, by functioning in our lives purely from the logical or conscious mind level, we do not see the full picture, nor do we access our full potential.

Intuition and inner guidance, on the other hand, is from the Universal Mind, and has access to an infinite data pool of all information, and is not limited to your own individualized data collection or beliefs, but is connected in a network of everything.

Imagine what could be possible, if you were able to make decisions based on this more expansive data pool, that is not limited to the capacity of the conscious mind but is unlimited, as your software has no viruses and therefore is unlimited.

It is through the software of the mind, that people like Einstein, Tesla and Mozart have made significant contributions to the world, through what some may call inspiration. But if we put it in simple terms, it is accessing a part of us that contains almost infinite files of data and has the processing capacity to analyze and interpret that data in a way that our conscious mind is unable to because of our limiting thoughts and beliefs.

By accessing the subconscious and Universal Mind through channeling, you are able to access data and interpret it in a way that, with the use of the conscious mind alone, would not be possible.

You can say that at a conscious mind level, at any given time as we live our day to day lives, we have a 10-degree opening to information due to the software that limits us. Channeling enables the possibility of widening this opening to be able to retrieve more information and hold a wider perspective than logic can. Not only are you able to access all the data in your own subconscious mind, but you are also able to plug into the Universal Mind and enter into a state of 'Oneness', where you are One and connected to everything.

Dira teaches one how to enter into this state of Oneness on

demand, like being able to flick a switch between being in this flow of Oneness and being in a state of logical reasoning. A poet, for example, may wait for inspiration to flow and have 'writer's block' without this technique, whereas Dira offers tools to be able to enter into the state of clear inspiration and intuition on demand whenever you want it.

2.7.6 HOW DO YOU EXPERIENCE CHANNEL?

So, to understand what is channeling? Channeling is the amplification of Divine energy within your being, and in that amplification of energy, there is the possibility for the experience of that Divinity through your senses.

So, it can be experienced through vision. It can be experienced through hearing. It can be experienced through sensations in the body. It can be experienced through you speaking. And the way that people channel differs, as you are all uniquely diverse. What is consistent is that there is a shift in energy, where you are aware of when you are in a conscious normal state, and when you are in a channel state, there is like a flick of a switch when the shift occurs.

So, what is this shift? This is the turning off of the conscious mind. So, are you consciously aware when you are channeling? You are consciously aware of what is happening, but you cannot interfere with what is happening, in the sense that if you are channeling words, so for example if you're channeling through speech, you cannot manipulate what is said with your words by your conscious thoughts.

So, your thoughts will be parked on the side. Your mental body, you could say, is observing what is happening, but it cannot override the channel. Does it mean that you are then out of control? No, because the channel always responds to your thoughts. So, if you have a question, or you don't agree with what is said in channel, the channel will respond to your question or your thought. OK?

If you want to get out of channel, you just need to think that you are done, and you will be done. So, it is not that you will be stuck in the state, and you cannot manage it. It responds to your conscious thought, but it's that the thought cannot interfere with what is happening in the channel.

2.7.7 ALL CAN CHANNEL

Channeling is a basic human capacity. There is no human being that is not able to channel. It is your basic human capacity, and the only limitation is the limitation of the self. It is the basic human capacity in the same way that you have a body, that you can move, that you can see, that you can hear, that you can walk, that you can talk, in the same way, you have the capacity to plug into the Infinite Source of Everything, because you are part of that Source.

The notion that this is reserved for specially gifted people is a delusion. Or that you have to be good enough, pious enough, religious enough? Also, a delusion, a mental construct. But the notion, of course, that there is a Supreme Source of Everything is a requirement, because the notion, that there is some form of Universal Consciousness, some Source of white light, and that you are a refracted version of that, is the requirement to be able to channel, and understand that you are plugging into that which is beyond you. You plug into everything as you are a part of that everything.

Refer to the following two pages for a Dira Map for Channeling Language & Expression, and a reflection sheet.

DIRA'S MAP FOR CHANNELING LANGUAGE & EXPRESSION

Reference Chart RC 011

PSYCHIC EXPERIENCE	EXPLANATION
CLAIRVOYANCE	Clear seeing. Where you see images or colors or visions in your mind's-eye and you are 'shown' something.
CLAIRAUDIENCE	Clear hearing. where you hear messages, sounds, guidance, and the inner voice is clear, as well as being able to hear sounds from the non-physical world.
CLAIRCOGNIZANCE / INTUITION/ INSIGHT	Clear knowing. Where you know something to be without having experienced it, it just is, like a download. Can be about the past, present or future, about you or anyone or anything else.
CLAIRINTELLECT / INSPIRATION	Clear thinking. Where you experience a download of information that your brain is not thinking, but it is an intelligent flow of data. So you may speak about things that your brain has never processed before.
CLAIREMPATHY	Clear emotion. In channel you can feel Divine vibrations like bliss, infinite love etc. Also where you feel another person's emotions as though you are one being, e.g you cry as you experience their sadness, but do not necessarily know why you are crying.
CLAIRSENTIENCE	Clear physical feeling. In channel, you can feel the energy of channel in your body and the vibrational flow, like how hot or cold, shivers or pulsations or an expansion of energy in your body. Also where you experience the physical sensations that another person feels, like pain in their body, you will feel it also as though you are one person.
CLAIRTANGENCY	Clear touching. Where you can feel the touch of things in the astral plane, like measuring and assessing the consistency & texture of energy, touching beings in the astral realm & feeling their touch etc.
CLAIRSALIENCE	Clear smelling. Where you are able to smell scents that are not in the physical world. That energy presents itself as a smell.
CLAIRGUSTANCE	Clear tasting. Where you can taste something without physically having it in your mouth.
AUTOMATIC WRITING	Where you draw or write without thinking, but it is just expressed through you.
XENOLALIA	Where you speak or write a foreign language including light language and verbalizing sound vibrations or song.
AUTOMATISM	Where your body moves in ways that you do not think of moving, or your physicality changes, for example you smile or sit up straighter, involuntary muscle contractions, etc.
AND MORE	Channeling is unique to everyone, there is no limit to the ways that this energy can be experienced by you.

ACCESSING DIVINE CONSCIOUSNESS

REFLECTION

When you tune into the deepest part of you, what comes up when you think about experiencing Divine?

2.8 COMMON QUESTIONS ABOUT CHANNELING

2.8.1 DO I NEED A GURU OR OBJECTS TO BE ABLE TO CHANNEL THE DIVINE?

No. There is no intermediary between any human being and The Divine, and using an intermediary whether a person, object, or image, is unnecessary and attributes the connection to something other than The Divine.

2.8.2 DO I HAVE TO BELIEVE IN GOD?

Dira assumes the perspective of Oneness, that everything is interconnected and Divinely orchestrated for a beautiful purpose, and the acknowledgment and belief in a Supreme Source of everything is a prerequisite to the experience. It is not associated with any particular religion or dogma, however the openness to experience the Supreme Universal Consciousness is necessary and accepting that everything in existence is energetically connected.

2.8.3 HOW LONG DOES IT TAKE TO LEARN HOW TO CHANNEL?

That depends on the person's openness to the experience. It can be instant, or not. It will happen when you are ready to listen and experience it. It is there for everyone, at any time, and any place.

2.8.4 DOES CHANNELING CONTRADICT RELIGION?

Channeling enhances connection, which is the intention of religion. This technique can be incorporated into all aspects of your life, including whatever form of worship you practice, if any. It is a tool to stop being distracted by your mind and thoughts, to enable clear access to the Supreme Being.

2.8.5 HOW IS CHANNELING DIFFERENT THAN PRAYER?

If you consider prayer as a way for you to speak to Divine, channeling is a way for you to hear the response from Divine, where your mental thoughts do not interfere in the communication.

2.8.6 HOW CAN GOD SPEAK THROUGH ME? ISN'T THAT ONLY FOR SPECIAL HOLY PEOPLE?

The Divine is always speaking through you and to you in the form of intuition and insight, the question should be 'Have you been listening?'. Channeling and connection to The Divine is not dependent on whether or not you are holy enough, or good enough; it is dependent on if you are ready to listen and be consciously aware of that connection.

2.8.7 CAN YOU DESCRIBE THE CHANNELING EXPERIENCE?

The Divine is the state of Oneness, and the human mind is in the state of duality. The experience of channeling the Divine as a vibration is that of bliss, infinite love, unlimited perspectives, and Omniscient guidance.

The manifestation of how channeling arises is unique to each individual as we are all uniquely diverse. Some people channel with their eyes open, some closed, some see images or light, others hear guidance, others feel a wave of energy, or have a knowing. You can be sitting, standing, lying down, or running, it is up to the individual to be in a state most comfortable to listen, but there will be a clear distinction when you enter into the state of channel as you will be in a state of Oneness, and the experience of that is different from a conscious mind waking state of duality.

The Divine will always communicate in the way that is appropriate for the individual.

2.8.8 WILL I BE AWARE OF WHAT IS HAPPENING?

In channel, you are consciously aware, but your thoughts do not interfere with the guidance. You may still have thoughts, but you will have an understanding or knowing what is your own thoughts and what is the Divine channel.

2.8.9 HOW WILL I KNOW THAT I AM ACTUALLY CHANNELING THE DIVINE?

The experience is blissful and there is no fear. If you feel fear or the guidance is perpetuating fear, then you are not in channel of The

Divine. Fear is the frequency of separation and duality.

2.8.10 IS CHANNELING THE SAME AS MEDITATION?

The goal of meditation is to reduce thought activity and silence the mind through varying techniques and is a practice. Channeling is the bypassing of thought to allow Divine connection using hypnosis, so it is quick, instant, and effective to quieten the mind and move into the expanded consciousness of Divine Oneness and the crown chakra perspective. Channeling can be used to enhance meditation or any other state of being where connection to The Divine is beneficial.

Furthermore, meditation focuses on you as 'the observer' that observes your thoughts. With channeling you can do that faster, but you move into an even higher level of consciousness of Oneness with Divine. In channel, by being connected to Divine, you experience the vibration, and your layers are released just by being in that Divine vibration, and you also receive clear guidance instantaneously and a wider perspective of your current situation.

Furthermore, in channel your energetic body becomes stronger faster, your vibration transmutes, and you are able to be in alignment more effectively.

3. DIRA CHANNELING INDUCTION

The channeling Induction is a guided meditation that brings you into a deep state of relaxation and visualization that opens the possibility of experiencing Divine as you enter into a trance state.

This process is safe and effective and is a requirement to experience all of the Dira programs and retreats. During the Induction, you will place a keyword, which will be your keyword to enter into channel in the future. Note that section A & H of this chapter is not channeled.

3.1 THE PROCESS OF CHANNEL INDUCTION

Now that you know what channeling is and that we channel Divine Source Energy at Dira, it is time to learn how to channel yourself. I am going to be your facilitator for the Dira Channeling Induction. And I'm very excited that you've made this decision to do this, and I hope that it will have a very positive impact on your life.

So, what is the reason why we have an Induction? So, the purpose of the Induction is so that you're able to enter into an experience of being in channel, that you don't need to keep on reliving that process to get back into channel.

So, the way that we teach channeling at Dira is that you're able to enter in and out of channel on command whenever you feel like it, just by using a keyword and setting an intention. So, this Induction is a way for you to get that keyword, so that whenever you want to channel in the future, you're able to just repeat the keyword three times, and set your intention to enter into channel of Divine, and then you are in channel. So, it speeds up the process and it becomes something that you can really integrate into your life so that you're not spending half an hour each time getting into that vibe, if that makes sense. So, this is why we have an Induction.

And the way we do the Induction is that it is a visualization technique where we use hypnosis. All you need to do is listen and follow the guidance of visualization. So, hypnosis is something that has been tried and tested at least since the sixties and it's a safe procedure. So, there's nothing for you to worry about. This process is very easy and safe. And if at any moment you feel uncomfortable, you can always stop, OK. It is a self-hypnosis. So, you are the one who's able to decide what you want to do. If you want to continue or if you feel uncomfortable at some point, you just stop the recording, and you can do it at a later time, if you want to. If you're interrupted for some reason during the recording, then you would need to start from the beginning and redo the Induction, because in order to get the keyword, it's important that you complete the full Induction.

The other thing is that if you fall asleep during the Induction, you will need to repeat it from the beginning, so that you can get the keyword, okay? Because the keyword is the last step of the Induction. And so again, just to reiterate, the purpose of the Induction is for you to be able to enter in and out of channel on your own command whenever you want to in the future, within about a minute or two. So, you won't have to spend half an hour each time getting into a deep state of trance. It will just be like an on-and-off switch. You say your keyword and you're in channel. Some people like to repeat the Induction so they can feel that Divine vibration or have that experience again, but it is not necessary to repeat it once you have your keyword.

And this Induction is a vibratory frequency. It's a vibration that you will experience. Okay, with this Induction, it is that you feel, what does it feel like to be in that vibration? So, if I was just to explain the process of the Induction so that you know what to expect because I'm assuming most people like to know what's going to happen. So, you can assume that you start with the breathing exercise. And in this breathing exercise, you're going to be inhaling and exhaling golden light, as golden light is the light of love. So, you're inhaling this love and then you exhale all of your stress, your worries, your limiting beliefs, etc. And then after the relaxation exercise, we start to take you through a standard hypnotic Induction with a staircase.

So, the way that hypnosis works is that you move from the conscious mind into the subconscious mind, and you start to enter into a trance. So, we're going to use the staircase and this staircase just takes you from the conscious mind into the subconscious mind, and you will be guided and counting down the steps to reach the corridor at the bottom of the staircase.

Once you're in the corridor, you're going to enter into a room. And in this room, this is really like the limiting beliefs; it's reflective of the limiting beliefs that you hold that prevent you from accessing that which is beyond your own physical reality. And you could say that we live in a physical dimension, but we also exist in a non-physical dimension, or what people say is beyond the veil, in some way. So, this room is going to enable you to clear the thoughts that limit you from accessing that dimension. And you're going to use light to clear it, and you will be guided to do that, and the mind is able to do whatever it is that it wants to do. So, even if you see things in the room, you just clear them out in your mind, and they will be cleared out.

So, it's a very simple and easy process. From that room, you're going to enter into a garden. And again, this garden is a standard hypnotic protocol for you to access that which is beyond your physical reality. And you could say, it's usually used by people to go to parallel lives or speak to guides or regress to prior to birth, as an example, to understand your soul. So, this garden is used a lot in hypnosis, and we're going to use this garden again, just to take you into that dimension where you are an energy being, but still refracted, still yourself. And then after the garden, we're going to take it a step further.

So, we then take you up an elevator to the sky. And this elevator is that - you're basically going to be entering into Source Energy. So, you move from a soul consciousness where you're separate, and you're going to move into this Universal Consciousness, where you're One with this light. So, you're going to exit the elevator and you just experience this white light of Divine. And this white light of Divine will be amplified and magnified, and you listen to this amplification, and you feel it in your body, in your experience, as this light becomes brighter and brighter. And then you're going to start to hear a song. And the reason we use this song is because sound moves beyond any language of what the mind would want to filter.

So, it moves beyond a language barrier, and sound vibration is very powerful; to be able to allow this vibration of this white light that you experience to merge into your being and to penetrate you fully so that you really feel this experience. So, when you hear the song, you just allow the vibration of the sound to penetrate your being. The song is The Song of Oneness. It is one of the standard songs that we use at Dira, and Oneness is that you are One with Divine. That is what Oneness is, it is the Oneness of you with Source. And so, it's that you're able to experience that you become this white light.

And once you experience that, then you're going to place a keyword. And this keyword is the word that you're going to use to bring you back into channel or to that experience. So, when you enter into channel, you're basically returning back to this experience of Source or Divine, this experience of white light.

And so, then you will have your keyword. And then in the future, when you want to channel, you just repeat your keyword three times. You set the intention that you want to channel, and you'll be in channel. So, the keyword is very important. You choose a word that you want that reminds you of that vibration and you can choose it while you're in the process. You don't need to think about it beforehand. You could if you want to, but you don't need to because it will become very clear to you when you're in that vibration. What is the word that comes up for you? And that will be your channeling keyword. And then the Induction is done. So, then you will come back to your body present in this time and space.

What is the other thing that's important? So, when you do this Induction, it's going to take you half an hour, and you need to be in a place that is quiet, where you don't have interruptions, and where your phone is on silent. If you're listening to this on your phone, make sure your phone doesn't have lots of beeps and messages coming through, and all of your notifications are silenced. Otherwise, it will keep on disturbing you through the process. Also, make sure you're not driving or doing anything that requires your focus because that will distract you from the process of the Induction. You don't need to be worried about whether you can do it correctly, whatever happens is what is perfect for you.

The Induction is one of the most important exercises that we offer at Dira. It is the foundation of everything that we do. In order to be able to enjoy all of our offerings, you need to have a keyword to enter into channel. After you've got your keyword, you will learn how to channel using the Dira Channeling Protocol. But for now, you focus on the Induction, so you can have your keyword.

So, get ready, get relaxed, and let's learn how to channel.

Refer to the following page for Dira's Protocol for Dira Induction.

PROTOCOL FOR DIRA INDUCTION

Protocol DP 001

OVERVIEW
- Be in a space where you feel you will not be distracted.
- Use this protocol for getting Keyword for channeling
- This Induction can be used by anyone who wants a keyword for channeling.

1. GOLDEN LIGHT BREATHING EXERCISE
- This is to prepare the astral body.
- You go through every part of the body, releasing debris and the burdens carried in that part of the body, by inhaling golden light and exhaling the shadow from that area.
- After the whole body and every organ is lit in golden light, you start to expand into the aura, the room, the building, the city, the country, the continent, the world, the universe, and past the universe.
- You keep repeating "The further you expand the brighter you become".

2. THE STAIRCASE
- To move you from the conscious mind into the subconscious mind.
- 20 steps going down.
- Brightly lit, with sturdy handrails on both sides.
- Starting with the left foot first, step down counting 20, 19, 18, etc. to zero.
- You are at the bottom of the staircase.
- If you cannot see the staircase, or it is not clear or scary, you have an entity, remove the entity using a mirror exercise or with a Dira Facilitator.
- If you see characters, just keep moving, you can channel later what they represent.

3. THE HALLWAY
- To move you towards the critical filter which is the room.
- You walk through a brightly lit hallway to the end, where you see a door, on the count of 3 you enter the room. 1, 2, 3 snap you are in the room.

4. THE ROOM
- Clearing the critical filter. (Removing blocks from entering deeper into the subconscious mind)
- Observe the room. It should be clear, empty, and bright.
- All contents, characters dirt, etc. are removed by a violet tornado of light that sucks up everything from the room and clears it completely.
- When the room is clear and empty, they walk towards the back of the room, to a door leading to a garden. On the count of 3 enter through the door into a garden, 1, 2, 3 snap - you are in a garden.

ACCESSING DIVINE CONSCIOUSNESS

PROTOCOL FOR DIRA INDUCTION CONTINUED

Protocol DP 001

5. THE GARDEN
- This is the universal mind of collective consciousness, but you are still in refraction (Soul consciousness).
- The garden can be familiar or unfamiliar.
- Look around and observe what you see.
- You will see a pathway that you walk along and follow.
- The pathway leads to an elevator.
- Step into the elevator.

6. THE ELEVATOR
- This moves you into Divine white light of Oneness (Divine consciousness).
- You see 12 buttons in the elevator, and press number 12.
- The elevator rises into the sky, and you count up 1, 2 , 3 , 4, 5... to 12
- At 12 the elevator doors open and they step out into BRIGHT LUMINESCENT LIGHT; this is the light of Divine, it is so bright, around you, in you, everywhere, all you experience is WHITE LUMINESCENT LIGHT.
- You magnify the light 1000 times on the count of 3. Count 1,2,3 snap the light is 1000 times more intense, it is so bright you feel it, you see it, this light of Divine.
- You magnify the white light again a million times, and then a billion times, repeating "It is so bright and intense", you feel it clearly, and you know this is the light of Divine Source Energy.
- Listen to the 'Song of Oneness', for the vibration to penetrate your being and feel this light and sound vibration intensely.

7. ANCHOR THE VIBRATION WITH A KEYWORD
- When you confirm that you feel the Divine light: "Now you will set a keyword, that whenever you repeat this keyword for the purpose of channeling, you will return directly back to this Divine white light experience, what is your keyword?"
- Then you anchor it by saying three times "Every time you repeat the keyword (insert their keyword) three times for the purpose of channeling, you will return directly back to this vibration of Divine. You repeat that 3 times to ensure it is anchored.

8. CLOSE CHANNEL
- Thank Divine for the blessings and guidance, and ask it to recede, while touching the heart chakra.
- "You may come back to your body, with all of your personality and consciousness fully present in your body in this time and space."

3.2 EXERCISE: DIRA CHANNELING INDUCTION

NOTE: The Dira Channeling Induction is a vibrational experience and includes The Song of Oneness. Reading the text of the Induction here will not offer the same experience as listening to it. To listen to the Induction, you need to have access to the Dira Basic Channeling Program, which can be purchased below.

DIRA BASIC CHANNELING PROGRAM

Welcome, and We're grateful for your presence.

We're going to take you through the Induction, and this Induction is a relaxation process that moves you from the conscious mind into the subconscious mind, and then into the Universal Mind.

So you find a place that is comfortable for you where you will have no interruptions for the next half an hour to 45 minutes. And if you have a phone, you put your phone on silent

And you just relax.

If you would like, you can keep your eyes open. And if you like, you can close your eyes. It doesn't make a difference.

And on the inhalation, you're going to breathe in this air, which is golden light. And on the exhalation, you release from your body any limitations.

So, you understand that golden light is the light of Divine love. And this light will transmute any low frequency vibrations within your body.

Allow this love to enter your being and release all of the debris and all of the energetic blockages.

You take a deep breath in, and you breathe this golden light into your head. And on the exhalation, you release all of your worries.

You take a deep breath in and feel this golden light lighting up your brain. And on the exhalation, you release all of the thoughts that are worrying you.

You take a deep breath in, and you allow this light to light up your eyeballs. And on the exhalation, you're going to release all the things you saw that you didn't want to see.

You take a deep breath in, and you allow this light to light up your ears. And on the exhalation, you release all the things you didn't want to hear.

You take a deep breath in and allow this golden light to light up your mouth. And on the exhalation, you release all the things you said that you didn't want to say.

You take a deep breath in and you feel this golden light lighting up the brain and the upper head, and on the exhalation, you're going to release all of the limiting thoughts that you hold.

You take a deep breath in, and your whole entire head lights up, and you exhale all of the debris within your head.

Taking another deep breath into the head, and you're going to feel the forehead lighting up, and on the exhalation, you're going to release any delusion that you hold.

You take a deep breath into the head, and you know that you can see clearly, on the exhalation.

Breathing into the throat. You allow this golden light to enter the throat on the inhalation, and on the exhalation, you release anything that held you back from expressing yourself fully.

You take a deep breath into the thyroid, and you exhale all of the things that you stopped yourself from living your full life.

You take a deep breath in, and this light starts to move down the right arm. And you feel this light going down the right arm all the way to the fingertips.

And on the exhalation, you're going to exhale all of the things that stopped you from doing what you wanted to do.

Again, breathing down the right arm all the way to the fingertips, this golden light, and you exhale all of the things that limited you from being who you want to be.

You're going to take a deep breath in and now this light is going to move down the left arm, all the way to the fingertips, and on the exhalation, you're going to exhale all of the things that stopped you from being happy.

Breathing down the left arm, this golden light is going to release all of the blockages from you feeling happy in your life, on this exhalation.

You breathe down this golden light all the way down both arms to the fingertips. And on the exhalation, you know that you can do and be whatever it is that you want to be.

You're going to breathe this light now into the chest, and you fill this chest with this golden light of Divine love. And on the exhalation, you're going to feel all of the sadness released from your body.

Take a deep breath into the chest and exhale your sadness. Breathing into the chest and exhaling your sadness.

You take a deep breath into the heart itself. And you exhale any conditions of love.

Breathing into the heart itself and you see all of the chambers of the heart light up. And you exhale any limitations that you have ever placed on loving yourself.

You're going to take a deep breath into the lungs, filling the lungs completely. And you're going to release all of the limitations for the love of life that you have.

You're going to breathe into the lungs again and you're going to release the stress of the world on the exhalation.

Breathing into the chest again, you're going to fill the chest completely with this golden light of love, and you're going to exhale any grief that you hold for those who you have lost, or those versions of yourself that you have had to leave behind. Breathing again into the chest and exhaling all of your grief.

You breathe into the back of the chest, all the way down the spine, and you're going to exhale all of the times that you felt unsupported. You breathe into the back and down the spine, exhaling all of the times that you felt unsupported or disappointed.

You're going to breathe into the abdomen. And as the abdomen starts to fill with this golden light, you're going to release on the exhalation, all of your anger.

You breathe into the stomach and you release all of the identity that you hold on to.

Breathing into your stomach, you're going to release control on the exhalation.

Again, the stomach is lighting up. On your inhalation and on the exhalation, you know that you are free.

And then you're going to breathe this golden light into your liver.

As the liver lights up in this golden light, you're going to exhale all of your bitterness and resentment. Breathing into the liver and the gallbladder. You release resentment and bitterness that you have held on to.

Breathing down into the pancreas, this golden light. And you release all limitations on the sweetness of life.

You breathe into the spleen, this golden light. Inhaling this golden light into the spleen. And on the exhalation, you exhale any limitations to feeling this vital life force within your being.

You're going to breathe this golden light into your intestines, and the rest of the digestive system, and you're going to release how you perceive the way you need to process or control your life.

Breathe into the entire abdomen, and on the exhalation, you know that you are free.

Breathe into the abdomen, and on the exhalation, you are comfortable with who you are.

You're going to breathe down into the pelvis and the sex organs, and as you fill the sex organs with this golden light of love, you're going to release any shame or guilt that you hold.

You breathe into the pelvis and the sex organs, releasing all of the energy of your partners and people who have imprinted in your life in a way that no longer serves you.

You breathe into the pelvis, and the sex organs, and you release any limitations on your creativity and your intention to offer this world your creation.

You breathe into the sex organs and the pelvis, releasing all frustration, all stagnation. Breathing into the sex organs and the pelvis, and you know on the exhalation, that you are here to offer this world an expression of Divine through you.

You're going to breathe down into the hips, and as this light starts to move down the right leg all the way to the foot, you're going to release on the exhalation any limitations on receiving nurturing from this earth.

You breathe down the right leg all the way to the foot, and you're going to exhale any tensions that you may hold with your mother.

You breathe down into the right leg all the way to the foot, and you see this light moving down into the earth as well, past the foot, as you receive the nurturing from the earth, as the earth is one with you.

You breathe down now into the left leg and feeling the left leg light up with this golden light of love all the way to the foot. You're going to exhale any limitations on feeling safe and secure.

You breathe down the left leg all the way to the foot, and you're going to exhale all of your fears.

Breathing this light of love down your legs, all the way to the feet, and on the exhalation, you know that you are safe.

Breathing down the legs, all the way into the feet and down into the earth, as this light spreads in the earth. And on the exhalation, you know that you can trust. You know that you are safe. You know that you are one, connected with this earth.

And as you continue to breathe in and out, this golden light of love on the inhalation and exhalation, you feel your body expanding beyond the surface of the skin. With every breath that you take in and exhale, you feel yourself expanding in golden light.

As you start to expand into the space where you are, with every inhalation and exhalation, you're going to feel yourself expanding in this light, into the chair where you are, into the room or place where you are.

And this golden light starts to merge in the golden light around you. This golden light is expanding from you, filling the air and filling the ground, and filling the building or the space where you are.

This golden light is going to start to spread and all of the inhabitants of the building, all of the rooms, the entire building or place that you are is going to light up in this golden light of Divine love. With every inhalation and exhalation, you feel yourself expanding further and further into the community where you are.

You feel the trees, the sky, the animals, and the earth, lighting up in this golden light of love that is radiating out of you. With every inhalation and exhalation, you feel yourself expanding further and further into the community.

Feel this expansion into the community in this golden light of love. As you are expanding into now mountains, into oceans, into cities and continents and countries, this golden light of love that you are is spreading throughout the earth so that the whole earth is a ball of golden light. This light of love that is radiating out of you.

And you feel yourself with the inhalation and exhalation expanding into the atmosphere, as you expand into the atmosphere and past the atmosphere of the earth, with every inhalation and exhalation, the brighter you become, the further you expand. You feel yourself expanding into the universe in this golden light of Divine love.

And the further you expand, the brighter you become. With every inhalation and exhalation, the brighter you become. Your light is expanding out into the universe, and you see this light lighting up the moons, the planets of the universe, as you expand further and further and past the universe, into the cosmos.

You see yourself expanding further and further, and the further you expand, the brighter you become, in this golden light of Divine love. Further and further past the universe, you are this infinite love.

And you're going to now just imagine that you are standing at the top of a staircase. The staircase is very well-lit and has very sturdy handrails going all the way down. You are at the top of a staircase looking down, and there are 20 steps. And starting with your left foot first, you're going to start to go down the steps.

20, 19, 18, 17, 16, 15, 14, 13, 12, 11, 10, 9, 8, 7, 6, 5, 4, 3, 2, 1. You're at the bottom of a staircase and you are in a corridor, and this corridor is also very bright and well-lit. At the end of the corridor, you're going to see a door and so you walk up towards the door. On the count of three, you're going to open the door and enter into a room.

1, 2, 3. You are in a room, and you just observe the contents of this room. Take note of what is in this room.

And now you're going to see a violet-purple tornado of light entering the room and sweeping up with it all of its contents except for you. Everything in this room is going to be swept up with this violet tornado of light as it sweeps up the contents and empties the room completely.

You are consciously aware that the room is completely empty, and you are the only thing in this room.

The room is empty. And at the back of the room, you're going to see a door that is leading outside into a garden. You walk towards the door, and on the count of three, you're going to exit through the door into the garden.

1, 2, 3. You are in the garden. And just take note of this garden. You observe this garden. It may be familiar or unfamiliar. It's okay. You just take note of what is in this garden. How does it feel?

And you're going to see a pathway, and this pathway is leading up to an elevator that goes up to the sky. You're going to walk along this pathway towards this elevator.

You have now reached the elevator, and in the elevator, as you enter, you're going to see 12 buttons. And you're going to press number 12, now, and the elevator is going to rise to the sky.

1, 2, 3, 4, 5, 6, 7, 8, 9, 10, 11, 12. The doors open, and you are in luminescent white light. As you exit the elevator, you are surrounded by this bright luminescent white light and this light is the light of Divine Source Energy.

This is the light of Divine. It surrounds you completely and passes through your being and interpermeates your body. Your entire experience is this white light of Divine.

Just feel this vibration. This light of Divine. It surrounds you completely. It is the only thing that you see, it is the only thing that you feel, is this white light of Divine Source Energy. And this light is so bright you can feel it within your being. You feel the intensity of this energy amplify with every breath.

With every second, it is becoming stronger and stronger and brighter and brighter. THIS LIGHT IS BECOMING STRONGER AND STRONGER AND BRIGHTER AND BRIGHTER. You feel this light so strong, interpermeating your being and surrounding you. It is within you, it is around you, it is you.

This light is becoming stronger and stronger and brighter and brighter. And on the count of three, it is going to amplify a thousand times.

1, 2, 3. The light is amplified a thousand times. It is stronger and brighter, stronger and brighter, and you know that this is the light of Divine Source Energy. This is the light of Source. This is the light of God.

It becomes stronger and stronger and brighter and brighter. And on the count of three, this light is going to amplify one million times.

1, 2, 3. The light amplifies a million times. It is the only vibration that you can experience in this moment. It is the light of Divine.

With every breath, you keep on breathing in and out, as it becomes stronger and stronger and brighter and brighter.

It is stronger and brighter, stronger and brighter, and on the count of three, it is going to amplify one billion times.

1, 2, 3. The light has amplified a billion times. It interpermeates your being and surrounds you and you feel it, intensely. And now you're going to ask for this energy to merge with you, to become one with you.

As you hear this song, this energy is going to merge with you and become one with you. You listen to this song, and if you feel called to, you sing along as well (The Song of Oneness).

And now you are going to place a keyword or a trigger word that every time you repeat this keyword, you will return back to this experience of Divine, and the merging of its energy with you. You're going to say this keyword out loud now three times.

Every time you repeat this keyword for the purpose of channeling, you're going to return back to this experience of Divine vibration.

Every time you repeat the keyword - and now you will say the keyword out loud now three times, repeat this keyword out loud now three times - every time you say this keyword for the purpose of channeling, you will return back to this vibration.

Every time you say this keyword three times for the purpose of channeling, you will return back to this vibration.

Allow the energy to settle. And just feel gratitude in the heart for this possibility.

Just feel this gratitude for this possibility. And you allow the energy to recede.

And you're going to come back to your body, fully present in this time and space.

You're going to feel now - you're just going to, on five, you're going to move your body slightly at the fingers and the toes. And at four, you're going to start to take a deep breath in, pulling your consciousness and the mental body back into the body.

At three, with the exhalation, you start to feel the ego returning, and the personality. At two, you're going to start to be able to move the body. And at one, your eyes are wide open, wide awake, with all of your personality and consciousness fully integrated in your body here and now.

5, 4, 3, 2, 1. Wide awake. You are fully present in this time and space, here and now, with all of your personality and consciousness present in this time and space.

3.2.1 TAKE A BREAK FOR PHYSICAL EXERCISE

Release the excess energy. Dance or jump for 5-10 minutes, so that your heart rate is elevated, and you mildly perspire. For every hour of channeling, you need to exercise for 10 minutes.

Note: You can play your favorite music, you don't need to judge if the music is spiritual enough.

 # REFLECTION

Take a few moments to reflect on your Induction.

1. Make a note of your keyword.
2. Note down the things you saw or felt during the induction.

3.3 WHY CAN'T I VISUALIZE ANYTHING IN THE INDUCTION?

The Induction process is built upon a standard hypnotic Induction, and the way that people assimilate data varies between one and the other. Some people are able to process data from a visual perspective, other people auditory, and others through senses or feelings. You could say that for someone who cannot visualize - what the question would be is: 'Are you able to feel it?'. So, for example, if you are at the top of the staircase, or the guidance is that you are at the top of the staircase, can you feel that there is a staircase there? That 'Yes, I feel that I am at the top of the staircase?'. So, this is the first aspect, is that for some people, the way that the brain functions, it is unable to visualize, and We will give a very simple test for you to be able to assess this.

So, if you just close your eyes for a moment.

And you just imagine that you're on a beach playing volleyball.

So, you just visualize or imagine that you're on a beach playing volleyball.

You look around and you see who is there.

What position are you playing?

What is the weather like? Etc.

Now you can open your eyes again, and you can assess. Were you able to visualize yourself being on the beach playing volleyball? If yes, then it isn't a problem of not being able to visualize. There is an issue related to resistance to the Induction.

And so, why would resistance arise? There are a number of reasons for that. One is that within your own belief system, perhaps there is a resistance or fear relating to channeling. The fears can be related to: Is this going to be something dangerous? Is it something scary? Is it something wrong? Will I be able to do it? Am I worthy of this? So, there are a large number of beliefs that can limit your capacity to be able to allow yourself to enter into this relaxed state.

And so, what We would say is that you ask yourself the question, or you write it down, or you even muscle test it. So, you can just stand up, and close your eyes. And you ask this cuestion as you're standing: 'Am I resistant to channeling?'. If you fall forwards, the answer is yes, and if you fall backwards, the answer is no.

So, if the answer is no. Then We will ask a second question: 'Is there something interfering with my energy that is blocking my connection? Or my capacity to channel?'. Again, you just feel - if you fall forwards, the answer is yes. And if you fall backwards, the answer is no. So, 'Is there something in my energy field that is blocking my capacity to channel?'. If the answer is no. Then you just understand that perhaps in the first Induction, there was some resistance. It means that there is no block, so, it's just - are you allowing yourself to fully experience this? And if the answer was yes, then we will need to allow for the release of this block or interference. Which We will deal with in the section about blocks. So, also with the question of 'Do you have a belief system that is blocking your accessing or entering into channel?'. Again, this will be dealt with in the section relating to blockages.

But this muscle testing technique, where you just stand up, close your eyes, ask the question, and you either fall forwards or you fall backwards. Falling forwards is the affirmative answer, and falling backwards is the negative answer.

What We would say is that usually those who are unable to see anything in the Induction, there is some kind of block in the crown chakra. And this block relates to fears, limiting beliefs about the relationship with being able to access this light or energetic interferences.

Refer to the following two pages for Dira's Protocol for Muscle Test, and a reflection sheet.

Protocol DP 033

# DIRA PROTOCOL FOR MUSCLE TEST

1. ENTER INTO CHANNEL
- Use pillar of white light (DP 002).
- Call on Divine using keyword.
- Feel shift in vibration.

2. MUSCLE TEST
- Muscle test can be done in a number of ways:
    - Standing: Ask the question, falling/ leaning forward means yes/affirmative; falling/leaning back means no.
    - Press index finger and thumb together. Using the other hand, try to separate them. If the lock holds it is a yes, if the lock breaks it is a no.
    - Note that for muscle testing, when the muscles are strong, it means yes/affirmative. Weak muscles mean no.

3. CLOSE YOUR CHANNEL
- Touch the heart chakra, expressing gratitude for this possibility by saying 'Thank you'.
- Close channel, asking the energy to recede.

REFLECTION

Muscle test the following beliefs relating to your ability to channel (DP 033):

- I am resistant to channeling.
- I am afraid of channeling.
- I have a belief system that is blocking my ability to access or enter into channel.
- I believe I am worthy of being able to connect with Divine.
- I believe it is possible for humans to be able to channel Divine.
- Is there something interfering with my energy that is blocking my connection? Or capacity to channel?

3.4 DO THINGS I SEE IN THE INDUCTION HAVE MEANING?

So, during the Induction, in the guidance, you will perhaps see many things that are not related to the guidance itself. In the breathing exercise at the beginning, it's unlikely that you will see anything that presents itself because the breathing exercise is about releasing what is within you.

When you start to move onto the staircase exercise, the staircase is reflective of that, which is, how you move from the conscious to the subconscious mind. And so, whatever you see on the staircase relates to your capacity, willingness, and beliefs, about being able to move from the conscious to the subconscious. So, for example, if someone is very mentally oriented and they don't believe in intuition or the subconscious mind, they may see things on the staircase that block it. So, for example, they may see that the staircase ends at a certain number. Or they may see that the staircase is very dark. So that just represents that there is a resistance to move into the subconscious.

If you see 'beings' along the staircase, or figures, etc. These are also representative again of energy related to moving into the subconscious mind. So, they may be energy interferences, or they may be just characters in your life that have told you - or implanted certain beliefs.

As you move in the hallway towards the room. This room relates to the chatter of the mind. That which is this filter of expanding the subconscious even further, or your accessibility to the subconscious mind. And so, if the room is full of things, it means that you have a lot of beliefs relating to your capacity to be able to access that which is beyond the veil, or that which is in intangible form, you could say.

What is important is that the room is cleared completely. It is not so important what you see. What is important in the exercise is that any of these blockages or debris are cleared as per the guidance of channel.

And then when you enter into the garden, this also relates to your, you could say again, beyond the veil experience. So, it doesn't really matter what you see, and perhaps you can - if you recall certain images, you can ask those images 'What do you represent?'. So, for example, maybe you saw images of guides or beings that want to help you on your journey or are assigned to help you on your journey, you can communicate with them through channel. But it isn't necessary, because if it is important for you to communicate with them, there will come a point where it will be very clear. The interface.

And then as you move up into the white light through the elevator, and come out in white light, some people may see other colors, they don't see white light. And this relates to your understanding of what Divine or God is. It relates to the notion that there is still some kind of separation. So if you are unable to see the white light, or you see other colors, you can understand that there is some sort of limitation in what you believe Divine to be, and how you are able to experience Divine directly without any form of intermediary, or the belief that Divine is not separate from you, is One with you, is something that you find hard to grasp. But does it really matter? No. What is important is that you are aware that this light at the end is Divine itself. And even if one has a limited understanding of what Divine is, the more that you channel, the more it becomes clear to you, the vast, infinite components of Divinity.

3.4.1 I SAW SCARY THINGS IN THE INDUCTION

So, what We would say is that it's the brain that decides if something is scary or not. It is a belief system. And therefore, it isn't something to be concerned about other than to recognize that it has presented itself to you because it's highlighting a fear that you hold. Is it important to deal with it now? Not necessarily. It's just to be aware that you hold fears relating to this process, or relating to being able to access that which appears to be intangible in some way. And eventually, these fears will need to be addressed, but they don't need to be addressed now.

Refer to the following page for a reflection sheet.

 **REFLECTION**

Digging deeper to understand what you saw in the induction:

1. Look back at your reflections from the induction. What were some of the things you saw that you want to understand further?
2. Go into channel of Divine using the protocol with your keyword and the pillar of light.
3. Call each image to be in front of you one at a time and ask them 'What do you represent?'. Keep asking more questions until you understand what they are showing you.
4. After you get the answer, thank it, and imagine a golden shower of light pouring down on you clearing all residue of energy of what you saw.

3.5 I HAVE FORGOTTEN MY KEYWORD - NOW WHAT?

So, if someone has forgotten their keyword, then they will need to do the Induction again. The keyword is very important so that you're able to enter into channel quickly in the future. The keyword is part of the development of this neural pathway in the brain that creates this pathway for easy access into the channel state or trance state, and without the keyword, then you just need to go through the whole Induction again.

3.6 FALLING ASLEEP DURING THE INDUCTION

So, if someone falls asleep during the Induction, they will need to repeat it. And the reason is because they need to be able to fully allow for the opening of the neural pathway in the brain so that it is established and created -you could say. And therefore, falling asleep during the Induction represents that you have resistance to be able to channel. There is some form of resistance. This is why one would fall asleep.

So, you could say, 'Oh, but I was so relaxed, and I just couldn't stay awake'. What We would say is that there is a perfect orchestration, of course, because when someone is resistant to something, they create the reality through their own orchestration to avoid that situation, as an example. And therefore, Our suggestion is you will need to do it again when you feel ready to embark on this journey. You can do it again immediately, or you can have some reflection and contemplation on what it is that you are actually resisting, and then you take the time to listen to the guidance once again.

But what We would say is that when someone sleeps through the Induction, it is the only channel exercise that must be repeated, because you can do other guided channel sessions where you fall asleep, and the energy works anyway. But the Induction is about clearing the neural pathway, and therefore it must be repeated until you are consciously aware of what is happening.

Refer to the following page for a reflection sheet.

REFLECTION

Falling asleep during the Induction:

1. Look back at your reflections from the induction. What were some of the first images or feelings you saw or felt before you fell asleep? They can give an indication of the block.
2. Close your eyes and see those images in front of you and ask, 'What do you represent?'
3. Wait for the answer.
4. Reflect below on the answer and decide if you are ready to move forward with channeling today.
5. If you are, repeat the induction.
6. If you aren't, listen to the rest of the program so that you are familiar with the process. You can always do the induction again in the future, and if needed with the help of a Dira facilitator to assist in clearing the blocks.
7. If you fell asleep during the golden breathing at the beginning, even before the staircase, try repeating sitting upright in a cool room, and actively follow the guidance of letting go of what you are guided to let go of. If there is something that you don't feel ready to let go of, you can say in your mind 'Not yet, when I'm ready', and continue following the rest of the guidance.

3.7 UNABLE TO FOLLOW THE INDUCTION INSTRUCTIONS

So, what We would say is that if someone is unable to follow the instructions, because they are too fast, or it is in a language that is not familiar to them, or for any reason that their cognitive mind is unable to process the data, then what We would say is that you listen to it the first time, so that you are comfortable with it, and then you do the exercise later on.

If someone is unable to follow the instructions for another reason, such as resistance, then We would say reflect on the resistance that you hold. This is not something that is compulsory for everybody to do. One makes a choice that they want to learn how to connect, how to experience this light. You're not forced to do this, and so if there is resistance within, then Our suggestion would be that you try to understand that resistance. And at times you could say that perhaps as an individual, you find it too difficult to really come to terms with the resistance that you hold. And then Our suggestion would be to, in a pair, that you channel together with someone who is more experienced and is able to guide you in releasing these resistances.

Issue with the Facilitation in the Recording

Dira has an online community and trained facilitators that speak many languages. If you would like to do the Induction in your native language, or with another facilitator, you can check to see if there is a facilitator offering that language.

Mental Block

Core Belief Release - to be done in a pair or with a Dira Facilitator.

Energetic Block

Entity Release - to be done in a pair or with a Dira Facilitator.

Refer to the following page for a reflection sheet.

 **REFLECTION**

Muscle test why you are unable to follow the instructions (DP 033):

- I don't understand the facilitator or English fluently.
- I don't like the audio recording.
- The instructions are too fast (I fall behind, I see ahead, I can't follow the pace of the breathing, etc.)
- I have a mental resistance to channel.
- I have an energetic block that prevents me from entering into channel.

Once you have muscle tested and understand the reason for the block, then you can look at solutions and see how you would like to manage it.

If you repeat the Induction and you still are unable to follow it, then you will need a facilitator to help you.

3.8 NEED MORE HELP WITH THE INDUCTION

Our goal at Dira is for people to have an enjoyable and effective channeling experience, so if you have questions or concerns that are not addressed here, please join the Group 'New to Channeling' on our Dira online platform and you can share your questions and experiences there with our community of channelers.

NEW TO CHANNELING GROUP

And if you feel that you would like a LIVE practice experience with an experienced Dira facilitator, you can book a private session or join a group-facilitated practice session.

BOOK A SESSION

4. CHANNELING PROCESS & GUIDELINES

Congratulations, you have completed the Induction, and now you are able to start channeling on your own by just using your keyword from the Induction.

4.1 TYPES OF CHANNELING AND WHEN TO USE THEM

There are different types of channeling, each with its purpose:

4.1.1 PILLAR OF WHITE LIGHT

The 'Pillar of Light' channeling is for receiving clear guidance and reception from Divine energy. It's important to note that the Pillar of Light channeling is not suitable for use when falling asleep. If you want to channel before sleep, you should use the Ball of Golden Light method instead.

- Chakras used: Crown and heart.
- Light color: Luminescent white light.
- Visual: Pillar of light in through the crown, out through the heart, and forms a pyramid of white light.
- Uses: To access Oneness, Divine guidance, Divine vibrations, and infinite library.
- When: A conscious decision to open & close the interface.

- **FOR ADULTS ONLY** *(it should not be used for anyone who has not yet reached puberty, as their energetic system will not be fully developed yet. Children that have not yet reached puberty can channel using the Golden Ball of Light protocol).*

4.1.2 THE GOLDEN BALL OF LIGHT

Another channeling method is called the 'Ball of Light'. This technique forms a protective shield of golden light, which serves to maintain your vibration and protect you from external energies that might affect you negatively. For example, if you know you'll be around someone who tends to bring you down energetically, you can use the Ball of Light to shield yourself from their negative energy.

- Chakras used: Heart.
- Light color: Golden light.
- Visual: Golden light radiates out of the heart forming a ball of light around you.
- NOTE: Can be used by children.

4.2 REQUIREMENTS OF CHANNELING

There are infinite ways that you can channel, but We are offering you a very efficient, effective way. And channeling is a part of the human capacity. You don't need to be good enough, or worthy of God, or vegetarian, or whatever it is that you think are the requirements to be able to be in Oneness. It is a part of the human capacity, and the reason it is a part of the human capacity, is again, it is an experience that enables the witnessing of your own Divinity.

So, in the channel you are witnessing white light, but by accessing the white light, you are able to witness your own spectrum of color. And in the process, you basically set aside, through a form of self-hypnosis, your thoughts, your emotions, your ego, and any interference, including physical interference.

So, for example, the room is noisy - does it disturb you when you're in channel? No. And so how is this done? It is done through a hypnotic Induction. Once you have passed through the Induction, and there is the placement of a keyword that will return you back to that state of Induction automatically, you then enter into channel for the first time.

And so, what We would say is that this process of Induction is for your brain to be able to perceive something is happening. Can it happen without this process? Yes. But as the mental body is active, in the provision of an exercise, there is the processing that it is occurring. With time, all of the visualization and whatever procedure you are given becomes irrelevant, and all you do is call on Divine.

So, then We would say what is the requirement of channeling Divine? It is to call on Divine, and you use the word that you feel comfortable with that is reflective of the Supreme Universal Consciousness, whatever word that is reflective of that which is the Ultimate Source of Everything. And you call on that to be known within you. That is channeling.

And then there are tools or aids to enable that process, which is through visualization and through a hypnotic trance Induction. But in essence, all it is, is the calling on Divine to be known within you.

4.3 PILLAR OF WHITE LIGHT (USES INDUCTION KEYWORD)

So, now what is the process of channeling that you have done the Induction and have your keyword? So, We are going to discuss the channeling process. There are many different ways to channel. Today We will be showing you two ways to channel.

The first is going to be with the pillar of light, and the second is going to be with a ball of golden light.

They have different functions. The first one We are going to discuss is the pillar of white light. We will explain what the process is, and answer questions about it and then you will experience it. And then you will practice it.

So, the process is, is that you activate two chakras. The first chakra that you activate is the crown, which is at the top of your head. So, the way that you do that is, you merely turn your attention to the top of your head. The second chakra that you're going to activate is the heart, and to do that you merely turn your attention to the heart, or you can touch the heart if you feel that you cannot pay attention to the crown and the heart at the same time. It is the activation of the two chakras simultaneously, the crown and the heart. And why is it two chakras? Because the crown chakra is for receiving, and the heart chakra is for releasing. If you only activate the crown, you become congested, because Divine vibration is the full spectrum of vibration, and what you are accustomed to, of your soul, is refracted spectrum of vibration. And so, when you open up the crown to receive this white light, and it flows through your body, it needs a release, and it is released through the heart. Is that clear?

So, you're going to first imagine that there is a pillar of white light. So, this pillar of light can be all the way up to infinity. But you can imagine, that as you look up, it is pretty far away, you cannot see the end of its source. Or you can just imagine that it is entering through the top of your head, and so you only see the area where it's entering, doesn't matter.

What you know, is that there is a pillar of white light that comes down from the sky, and it enters through the top of your head, and as it enters through your head, it starts to light up your body, and you can visualize or feel it lighting up your body. And when it reaches the heart level, you feel it like a valve releasing this white light. As it releases the white light, it starts to push away your mental and emotional bodies.

So, the light enters through you, and as it does, it is released out of the heart, and you feel to some degree that this light is expanding out of you. And you can assume that as this white light expands out of you, it removes all of your interfering thoughts and emotions.

And then you will form a pyramid of white light around you, and this pyramid is to ensure that you feel confident that nothing is going to enter into your space except Divine vibration. And when We say nothing will enter, that includes your thoughts. So, the reason why it is pushed out of you is because you are pushing out the mental body and parking them outside of this pyramid. If you cannot see a clear pyramid, and you just see that you're in white light, it is just as good, because you know that you are in this white light, and nothing will enter into the white light. Is that clear?

The next step is you call on God. You call the Divine, whatever you want to call it, that is reflective of the Ultimate Source of Consciousness. And what We would say is, that terms such as the Higher Self, which is reflective of the soul, is not the Ultimate Source of Everything. Also, terms such as 'The Universe' is a part of the creation of the Ultimate Source of Everything, it is not the Source of Everything. And so, although in media it has become common to use terms such as 'The universe has done this for me', the universe, is in actuality, the creation of the Omnipotent. And so, you are limiting yourself, and this exercise is to access the Ultimate Source of Everything.

So, you use the term that you feel comfortable with, it can be Source Energy, it can be Universal Consciousness. It can be the Divine. It can be Elohim, God, Allah, or whatever you want to name this Ultimate Source of Everything. But that in your perception, you know that there is nothing beyond this. And you keep on calling on that. To make itself known within you. And you allow the shift in vibration to occur.

So, what will be done in the Induction, is that you will experience this vibration through the Induction, and then you will be planting a keyword. And so, We will say you will now use a keyword, and this keyword will return you back to this experience of Divinity whenever you repeat it three times. So, you remember what this keyword is, and when you are now going to channel, you can alternate between saying the keyword, and 'I call on Divine Source Energy or God', etc. You keep on repeating your keyword and calling on Divine until you feel the shift in vibration.

4.4 CLOSING YOUR CHANNEL

You close it just by expressing gratitude. So, you can say 'Thank you' and it will recede or close. If you still picture it there, then it will be maintained, so you imagine that it also dissolves or goes away.

It is not that there is a danger, it is just that there is the opening of the crown, and in the opening of the crown, there is, depending on one's perspective of susceptibility, as it is a mechanism for communication, there may be communication where you are not consciously aware that it is a Divine vibration.

So, for example, if you are asleep, your conscious awareness is not alert, and therefore, as the crown is open, there is a possibility of you having dreams or nightmares as an example. Some people like to have dreams or nightmares, but what We would say is that you do not need to wait until you are asleep to be able to have clear communication, you just need to listen.

The reason why people feel comfortable with seeing something in a dream is that they recognize that it has nothing to do with their conscious thought, and therefore must be some form of message or processing. But you can also be in a wakeful state, as has been experienced, where you are in channel, and you have clear communication, and conscious thought is not interfering.

Refer to the following page for Dira's Protocol for White Light Channeling.

DIRA PROTOCOL FOR WHITE LIGHT CHANNELING

Protocol DP 002

OVERVIEW
- Be in a space where you feel you will not be distracted.
- Use this protocol for receiving messages, vibrations, accessing Oneness, and guidance from Divine
- DO NOT use for children, or people on psychotropic drugs or affected/ blocked crown chakras.

1. HEART ACTIVATION
- Gently touch the heart chakra in the center of the chest to activate the heart chakra.
- Feel GRATITUDE for this possibility of union and connection with Divine.
- Gratitude to Divine: "Thank you Divine Supreme God, for your great blessings, guidance, and protection."
- Set the intention to connect to Divine in your mind.

2. ACTIVATE THE CROWN CHAKRA
- Focus on the top of the head to activate the crown chakra.
- Be open to receiving this Divine light & guidance.

3. IMAGINE THE WHITE LIGHT
- Imagine a pillar of luminescent white light coming down from the sky and entering through the top of your head.
- The white light enters through the head and fills the head, neck, shoulders, arms, chest, abdomen, pelvis, down the legs all the way to fill the feet.
- Stay focused on this white light so that the whole body is filled with white light.
- Imagine or instruct the white light to become brighter and brighter. You can say to the light: "Amplify, stronger brighter".
- You are completely filled with bright white light.

4. THE LIGHT RADIATES OUT OF THE HEART
- Imagine or feel the white light radiating out of the heart chakra (center of the chest).
- This white light radiating out of you expands to form a pyramid of white light around you.
- You are completely within this pyramid.
- Nothing of a vibration other than Divine white light can enter this pyramid, and it pushes out all vibrations within you that are not a match to this white light as well.

DIRA PROTOCOL FOR WHITE LIGHT CHANNELING CONTINUED

Protocol DP 002

5. SET INTENTION
- Set intention to connect to Divine through channel.
- Say 'I call on Divine to be known to me' or use the word you feel comfortable with that refers to Divine Supreme Consciousness.

6. SAY YOUR KEYWORD
- Say your keyword 3 times to enter into channel (from the induction).

7. REPEAT
- Repeat steps 5 and 6 until you feel a shift in vibration and you know you are in channel.

8. ALLOW THE CHANNEL TO MAKE ITSELF KNOWN
- Allow the channel to make itself known to you by showing you a sign, like a physical sensation, or by saying a welcome phrase.

9. QUESTIONS
- Ask the questions you want out loud.
- For example, say out loud '(your name) ... is asking ....?'
- Allow the channel to respond to your question. You may experience the answer in many different ways, be open.
- Always speak out loud when channeling, even if it is to ask a question.

10. CLOSE CHANNEL
- Thank Divine for the blessings and guidance, and ask it to recede.
- You say 'Thank you' while touching the heart chakra to emphasize gratitude.

4.6 QUESTIONS ABOUT CHANNELING

4.6.1 ARE THERE ANY RITUALS TO CHANNEL?

Is there some form of ritual required to channel? No. If one feels more comfortable doing all of their rituals, then they are free to do so. And if one doesn't feel like doing it, they are free to do so. All it takes is the flick of a switch, in that the conscious mind is surpassed or subsided.

4.6.2 CHANNEL IN THE NATURAL WAY FOR YOURSELF

So, what We would say is that you don't need to dictate how it should look, or how you should be, whatever unfolds naturally for you, is natural for you. So, if your eyes are open, then they are open. If they are closed, then they're closed. Don't think that it needs to be a certain way. Just allow it to unfold in the most comfortable way, the most natural way for you.

Participant: Can you see the physical world when you channel?

A: It depends on you, and it depends on what is the purpose of the channel. So, for example, for Lubna, if her eyes open, sometimes she sees only light, sometimes she sees vague figures, and sometimes she sees something very specific of what is in front of her. It depends on what needs to be seen. So, when you're in channel, it is not like normal eyesight, it is Divine's eyesight. So, do you need your eyes to be open or closed to see with Divine's eye? Even if it is closed, you will still see with Divine's eye, because it is not the eyeball that enables sight.

So, do you need to be sitting? Do you need to be lying down? Do you need to be standing? Do you need to be jogging? You don't need to be doing anything, whatever is comfortable for you, what enhances your channel - do it. If you feel that when you go jogging your channel is stronger and clear, then go for a jog and channel while you're jogging. You don't need to be sitting in a quiet place, you can be in a very noisy place and still be able to channel. There are no conditions. Just be alive, that's all.

4.6.3 WHEN TO CHANNEL

So, how often should you channel? As often as you like. Can you channel all day? Yes. Can you channel once a day? Yes. Can you channel once a year? It's up to you. But to be in connection with Divine energy is blissful. And it changes your life to be more blissful. So, don't feel that if you have a question, it's not important enough to go into channel for. Should I paint my fingertips red or violet? You can even ask that in channel. There is no question that is insignificant to ask.

When you shouldn't be in channel? It depends on what sort of channel you're referring to. So, the golden ball of light, you can be in it all the time for your entire existence. With regards to the pillar of light, it is a conscious state, it is a conscious connection. So, if you are not in a conscious state, then it is not appropriate to be in that form of connection. For example, if you are completely intoxicated, it is not appropriate to be in that state, because then you will have a distortion of the channel, and then you will blame Divine for giving you the wrong information when it is merely you are not in a conscious enough state to be in channel for guidance.

But to feel the vibration, it can be all the time. Is that you can't go to the bathroom and be in channel? Of course, you can do anything you want. We created you. It is not about space or activity; it is about the degree of your conscious awareness. Does it need to be quiet to be in channel? No. Do you need to sit a certain way? No. Do you need to wear certain clothes? No. Is there a ritual? No.

What We would say is that the only reason why someone would not be in channel when they want to be in channel is because it serves them in some way to not be in channel, and this way of serving them can have infinite reasons. So, for example, it is a part of their journey, in this nurturing of this relationship, or discovering. It could be that they have other frequencies of vibration that they are very comfortable with, that if they go into the channel with the Divine, they will lose these lower frequencies of vibration, and so it serves them to stay in the low frequency of vibration. Does that make sense?

So, We will give the example of people who have 'guides', they call them guides, it's just an energetic being, as an example. If the guide is interfering with the channel, the only reason why you would not be able to go and channel is because you don't want to lose the guide, but to get into channel, the guide needs to go, because the channel is what is meant to be dominant. Does that make sense?

It can be spiritual guides, it can be angels, it can be demons, it can be anything. But if it serves you to hold on to that frequency of energy, that is what will stay, because that is what you choose. So, for example, you could say, that someone feels very powerful because of this guide, or because of this energetic being. And they'll say, 'Oh but this was passed to me from my ancestors, and I'm very special because I have this being'. So, then We would say, well why are you here if that is what serves you?

We are not going to compete with lower frequencies of vibration. And if someone chooses to channel lower frequencies of vibration, that is their choice, and it is OK. But there should not be the contradiction of saying that they want to channel Divine, when in actuality, they are holding on, and very comfortable with this other frequency of vibration.

So, until they are at the point where they actually want to release that association, then they will be able to channel Divine. Does that make sense? And from an energetic perspective, it is very clear. So, when there is a connection to lower frequency vibration other than Divine Source Energy, the crown chakra is blocked. The first step is releasing them.

4.6.4 CAN I ASK CHANNEL ABOUT ALL ASPECTS OF MY LIFE?

There is no part of your life that you can't ask about. You can ask about the past, present & future as all are One in the Oneness of Divine. You may be shown what is the most highly probable at that moment in time and what is most important for you to know for your soul's journey of witnessing at that point in time. What is always important is to channel about it from a Divine frequency of vibration, in Divine channel.

And then the question comes, 'When am I ready, when am I enlightened, is it when I start channeling?'. One needs to understand, what does enlightenment imply, that a human is only light? If that were the case they would not be in a physical body, or no longer need to be incarnated in a physical body. You can have moments of alignment and being in your light, but it is a constant fluctuation of energy, you do not stay in one state. Every thought you have changes your energy field, every emotion, all environmental influences, for example. So, channeling helps to remove the layers of staying out of your light, or dimming your light, but because Divine is infinite, you never fully let go of everything, because infinite means, by definition, that there is no end to how bright you can become.

What We would say is, if you were to imagine it like a flower, so today you say these are my issues - the outer petals, and they fall. And then there are petals also in the next layer, and then they fall. And then there are petals inside, and they fall, and then they eventually get to the pollen or the nectar, which is your beautiful soul. And so, you have a lifetime, for experience. You shouldn't think of it as 'Now I am fixed and perfect!'. You are perfect anyway. But through every experience you have, you are witnessing Divinity through different perspectives.

Also, to note, the way channeling has evolved, or being able to access this Divine consciousness through intention has evolved over time, as collective consciousness starts to elevate.

So, what We would say is that, through the experience and capacity to channel, there is the capacity to channel anything, including that which is not Divinity. So, for example, in the opening of this possibility, that there is the plugging in, or the tapping into a frequency of vibration of Source Energy, there is also the possibility of plugging in or tapping into energy that creates layers. Does that make sense? So, if you are in clear Divine channel, then it will only be that which is beautiful, blissful, and beneficial for humanity.

But there is also the possibility that because someone is channeling, energy can be manipulated for the use of the ego. Does that make sense? So, in the same way, you did the ball of light earlier where you were able to form a ball of light by your mere thought, you can also form many things with mere thought. Does that make sense?

And so, in the past, you could say hundreds of years ago, as an example, there was an awareness of course that humans had the capacity to be able to tap into that which was 'unseen' or 'energetic forces'. And then those energetic forces, because they were not using or accessing the Ultimate Source of Energy, there was manipulation.

So, for example, there was, you could say, in the manipulation or exchange with lower frequency beings, especially because there is the belief that you are not able to access God, and then you use an energetic being instead, then there is, from the frequency of control of the solar plexus, the end result is not a magnificent unfolding.

And because the dominant collective consciousness at that time was sitting in the solar plexus, it was understood by those who were Divine channels, that as a collective consciousness, this could be manipulated in some way. So, for example, you could say that if there was a saint or a guru who was teaching his followers, there was a trickling of information in the assessment of whether or not they were on the path beyond that of the solar plexus you could say. And is that required now? What We would say is that, as a collective consciousness, there will be transmutation of vibration away from the solar plexus to that of the heart. Is everyone in humanity at the level of the heart at the moment? No. And so, when We say that you were here today for a reason, it is because you are ready to operate at this Divine frequency.

And it is not about convincing others of how to behave, or when they will be quote-unquote 'ready', but if they choose to persist in a frequency of vibration because it is comfortable for them, then they can continue in that frequency because that frequency is also to be witnessed and experienced. There is nothing right or wrong about that. Does that make sense?

So, to keep in mind that when you are channeling, you channel Divine Source. You can ask any question you want, but make sure it is Divine Source, not some other being or energy.

4.6.5 HOW DO I KNOW THAT I AM SAFE WHEN I CHANNEL?

So, for you to know that you are safe when you're in channel - and We assume that this implies about low frequency vibrations entering into your channel - so, the reason why you activate the heart is that you allow the vibration of channel or Divine light to radiate out of you from the heart, forming this pyramid of white light around you. And this pyramid of white light around you acts as a shield from any low frequency vibration from entering into your field. It is important to follow this process. We understand that as people become more experienced with channel, then they decide to take shortcuts, perhaps avoiding steps, but We will reiterate that it is important to follow the protocol, so that you can always rest assured that everything will be safe, and you are held in Our embrace.

Would it be, that if you don't create the pyramid of white light around you, that you are not safe? That is not what We are saying. What We are saying is that the pyramid of white light has a purpose, otherwise it would not have been included in the protocol. And this purpose has many functions, one of which is to create a shield or a barrier to low frequency vibration. And other purposes are, as an example, for the amplification of energy. But if you follow the protocol correctly, there is nothing to fear at all. You are One with Us and We are One with you, and it is a natural capacity of the human to be able to access Our field of white light.

4.6.6 WHAT DETERMINES THE CLARITY OF CHANNEL?

So, one would say 'I did yoga for twenty years, is my channel going to be clearer than someone else?', no. The clarity of the channel is based predominantly on your own intention of connection.

So, how does connection take its form? The intention to connect with the Divine, as well as the intention to connect with that which is around you. If there is a clear request for disconnection in your intention, then your channel will not be clear. Is it to say that you will not be able to channel at all? You will be able to channel, but there will be distortion.

So, again with the process of channeling, in order to enhance the channel, it depends on the intention of connection. And that which distorts the channel is that of intentional disconnection.

And what does intentional disconnection mean? For example, latching on to judgments, or the assumption that you are separate from someone else as an example. Or the assumption that your identity is superior to that of others, as an example. Because in the identification with the ego so strongly, for example, 'I am the superstar and now I can channel, everyone else is just mediocre' - not knowing that you separate yourself. Does that make sense?

So intentional separation from the Self, the Divine soul aspect of the Self, when one is very judgemental of themselves, feels unworthy of this connection, identifies with the mental body to the point that there is a dismissal of this possibility of Divine guidance and connection; the channel can be distorted. Furthermore, extreme emotions can also distort the channel. Therefore, the maintenance of balance and clarity of the energetic system is important. One needs to feel worthy of this connection and have full faith and conviction that it is possible.

Everyone channels somewhat differently. The way that it is magnified is individual. It is when you feel most unlayered and relaxed. Most yourself. Because what is the channel? It is the realignment to the Self, and in the realignment to the Self, there is the plugging into the Ultimate Source of Everything, and shifting into that perspective of Oneness, away from the perspective of the ego, or the mental body or the emotional body.

So, what are some other things that impact the energetic system, that also impact your capacity to channel? Well, the use of psychotropic drugs cracks the aura and therefore enables the flow of that which is not within your full intention, to enter, or leave your space. It's the same with intoxication in extreme amounts. It cracks the aura, and therefore the maintenance of vibration becomes difficult. Is it to say you can't have fun? Of course, you can have fun. But it is to understand and have the conscious awareness of at what point do you become impacted, and that the clarity of your channel becomes distorted. Does that make sense?

So, are We saying that you cannot drink? That is not what We're saying. What We are saying is you have to have conscious awareness of your own faculties, and you know your limits.

With regards to psychotropic drugs - it is not possible to channel clearly with the use of psychotropic drugs using the pillar of white light protocol. Anyone who is using psychotropic drugs needs to use the ball of golden light protocol, and in the ball of golden light, they are only able to feel the vibration, it is not for guidance.

So, for example, if you stop the psychotropic drugs, then you are able to rebuild the aura in its full form? Yes, and it does not take long to do, and then you're able to channel clearly. But of course, you can't stop the drugs or medication unless you are advised by a medical practitioner, if it is for medicinal purposes.

And if one finds that they cannot channel clearly, then you can refer to the section on releasing blocks or get assistance from an experienced facilitator.

4.7 PHYSICAL EXERCISE REQUIREMENT WHEN CHANNELING

We will speak briefly about the reason for the physical movement after channeling, aside from having fun. So, if you were to imagine, just from a normal perspective of science, of what has been understood, the process of breathing enables elements to enter the body, such as oxygen, be reintegrated into the blood, circulated around the organs, and the debris released, in the form of carbon dioxide. So, you can say that you have a scientific explanation, as to how Divine life-force flows through you.

If you were to look at it in a different way, as you inhale air, you inhale Our love, as Our love interpermeates everything, and you are consuming something that you perceived to be separate from you, and this thing that is separate from you, is love that interpermeates the air. So, you breathe this love into your body. This love spreads around your body and is circulated around your energetic system. And in that process, it collects with it debris and layers, and things that are blocking your light from shining, and on your exhalation, you release the debris or shadow.

So, from one perspective you could say, that the purpose of breathing and your circulatory system, is to ensure from a scientific perspective that your body is oxygenated. From another perspective, you can say that breathing is a process in which you can integrate Divine love within you, for the purpose of transmutation. In the same way, when you eat you also ingest Divine love, that transmutes you, and then is released with its debris. So, the systems of the physical body are not separate from an energetic system in its purpose.

We had mentioned that Divine light enters through you, transmutes you, and is released. And physical exercise is a part of the maintenance of your temple, and this body, this gift that you have been given for physical experience, in that when you channel, the intensity of your channel is dependent on the circulatory system, the flow of the blood, the capacity of this love to flow through you, and through your body. Makes sense?

And so, if you have, for example, a disease in an area of your body, then this flow becomes blocked. So how do you enable this flow to open? It is by channeling a measured portion of Divine vibration that will slowly transmute it, or quickly transmute it, but that the intensity of the frequency will be measured for what your physical body can handle.

So, what We would say with regards to once you are in channel, the vibration can be intense, and so physical exercise is necessary if you are in channel for prolonged periods of time. You can consider that for every hour that you are in channel, you should do at least 10-15 minutes of physical exercise where you are increasing your breath and perspiring to some degree. It is important so that you do not become congested. When the body becomes more acclimatized to being in channel, then the requirement for the exercise reduces somewhat, but you would still need to exercise because as you become accustomed to channel, the intensity of the energy increases.

So, you can say that on the first day that you channel, you can feel like a candle that lights up, maybe after one year, you feel like a big flood light has lit up. It intensifies in its vibration. And from an energetic maintenance perspective, the preparation of the physical body is important. It is important, especially when you are doing this on your own, to keep that in mind.

So, for example, when someone channels, and then they say, 'I have a headache, or my chest hurts, or my legs feel uncomfortable'. It's because there's debris in those areas, and the congestion builds up, and it needs to be released. So, if you feel any physical discomfort after channeling, all you need to do is a little bit of exercise or movement. It doesn't mean you have to hit the gym; it just means that you need to release the congestion. And you assume a correlation, for every hour of channel, at least fifteen minutes of exercise. When the body becomes more accustomed to a higher intensity of vibration, then you can exercise less. But as you are adjusting to the intensity, you ensure that you are always in a normal comfortable state.

What We would suggest, is that, as you are starting to channel, that you shouldn't stay in channel for more than an hour, as congestion will accumulate, and you will start to feel uncomfortable. The physical body needs an acclimatization to this frequency as it has been used to being clogged with debris, and with the cleansing of the system, the body takes time to adjust.

4.8 EXERCISE: DIRA CHANNELING PROTOCOL AFTER INDUCTION

Try to channel on your own now by following the Channeling Protocol.

Note: Channeling is a vibrational experience. Listening to the audio recordings is not equivalent to reading the script here. To access the audio recordings, you will need to have access to the Dira Basic Channeling Program.

DIRA BASIC CHANNELING PROGRAM

So, you just relax and get comfortable.

And you're going to start by just placing your hand on the heart chakra, activating the heart chakra.

And as you activate the heart, you just feel gratitude for this possibility of connecting with Divine.

Just feel this gratitude filling the heart, as the heart chakra becomes larger and larger.

And you say in your mind, 'I'm so grateful for this possibility'.

And then you're going to focus and turn your focus to the top of the head, to the crown chakra. And just allow it to open.

You instruct the crown chakra to just open.

And as it opens, you see or visualize, or feel a pillar of white luminescent light coming down from the sky that is entering through the top of your head.

You see this pillar of white luminescent light coming down from the sky.

It is entering through the top of your head, lighting up your body.

It lights up the head, down through the neck, into the shoulders.

Past the shoulders, down the arms, and the chest.

Into the full torso, filling the chest and the abdomen, all the way to the pelvis.

Filling the pelvis and the hips, and then down the thighs.

Past the knees, all the way down the legs, to the feet.

There is a pillar of white luminescent light coming down from the sky.

It is entering through the top of your head, lighting up your body.

Feel the whole body lit up with this luminescent white light.

There is a pillar of white luminescent light coming down from the sky. It is entering through the top of your head and lighting up your body, and you see this light filling your body.

And you're going to see it radiating out of the heart as it starts to form a pyramid of white light around you, and you imagine, or visualize that you are completely sitting within this pyramid of white luminescent light around you, as it has pushed out all frequency of vibration that does not reflect this vibration of Divine white light.

You imagine this pyramid around you of white light. As you are almost in the solid white light within this pyramid. It is so bright and intense.

And on the count of three, it is going to amplify a million times.

1, 2, 3. The brightness of this pyramid of light and the light within your body is going to amplify a million times.

Just see it becoming so bright and intense and feel this vibration of light.

And then you're going to say in your mind, 'I call on Divine to be known to me'.

And you repeat your keyword three times NOW.

'I call on Divine to be known to me'. And you repeat your keyword three times.

And you keep on repeating this until you feel the shift in vibration.

'I call on Divine to be known to me' repeating your keyword.

When you feel the shift in vibration, you're just going to say 'Amplify, amplify, become brighter, stronger, more intense. Show me your presence within me. Brighter and stronger. More intense, I call on Divine to be known to me'. Repeat your keyword.

'I call on Divine to be known to me' and repeat your keyword. And you are in channel. Just take note of this vibration and what it feels like.

And when you are ready, you thank this vibration, and you say in your mind 'You can recede'.

Just place your hand on the heart chakra in gratitude for this possibility.

And when you are ready, you come back to your body fully present in this time and space, with all of your personality and consciousness fully present in this time in space, here and now.

Refer to the following page for a reflection sheet.

 **REFLECTION**

Reflection R 008

Practice channeling on your own:

1. Write down some questions that you want to know from channel. Start with 3 yes or no questions and 3 other questions. One of the questions should be 'How do I know that I am in channel?'.
2. You can record these questions on your phone so that you can hear them, and that your mind doesn't need to be occupied with trying to verbalize or remember them. If you don't have a phone, you can also say '(insert your name) ... is asking ...?' when you are already in channel, so that you differentiate between your mind and the answer of channel.
3. Record yourself when you are in channel using your phone or computer so that you can capture the answers in case you forget them once out of channel.
4. Verbalize the answers from channel out loud. Even if you see an image, describe the image out loud. Describe everything that you feel and see out loud.
5. When you are done channeling, make some notes about your experience.
6. Make sure to do some physical exercise like jumping jacks or dancing for 10-15 minutes for every hour that you are in channel.
7. Ask questions in the Dira 'New to Channeling' Group on the Online Platform if you have any or want to share your experience. Also, if you are looking for a partner to practice with, mention it in the group.

4.9 HOW DO I KNOW I AM IN CHANNEL?

So, once you have finished the Induction exercise, you will then do the channeling process. And in the channeling process, it is how you would channel on your own, by activating the crown and the heart, imagining the pillar of white light coming down, radiating out of the heart, and forming the pyramid of white light around you. In that process, you set the intention that you say, 'I call on Divine to be known to me'. It is this intention that creates the connection. So, what We would say is that as soon as you set that intention, from a Divine perspective, you are already in channel, because the intention itself is the trigger on the calling of that consciousness to be present within you.

The issue only comes if you are not aware of that connection. From Our perspective, We are always connected with you, and once you have set the intention by saying 'I call on Divine to be known to me', We automatically amplify Our presence. So, it is only that, do you know that We are present? Are you consciously aware of Our presence? And there are signs to be able to communicate that to you. And that is why one of the first questions you ask of your channel is 'How will I know that I am in channel?'.

These signs can be physical signs, in the sense that you feel a fluctuation of energy within the body. You feel a tingling sensation somewhere in the body. You can feel hot or cold sensations. They are physical signs that may show you that you are in channel. Your breath may change, your heart rate may change, as an example. For some people, there is no physical sign, but there is a knowing or presentation, or communication through the mind - in the sense that there may be words that you hear of Us communicating through you, a vision that you may see, such as color or flash of light, or other sorts of ways that data is presented to you, so that you become aware.

And the third way, as We have mentioned, because each person learns and experiences the world differently, with a different emphasis of their senses, the third can be just with the knowing of Our presence. So, what We would say is that you ask, once you have gone into channel, 'How do I know I'm in channel?', and then you can say 'Amplify this 1000 times'.

So, We will do the exercise now.

So, you enter into channel,

There is a pillar of white luminescent light coming down from the sky, it is entering through the top of your head, lighting up your body.

And it starts to radiate out of the heart.

Then you call on Divine to be known to you.

You say, 'I call on Divine to be known to me', and you repeat your keyword three times.

Allow for this shift of vibration.

And on the count of three, this vibration is going to amplify 1000 times.

1, 2, 3. It has amplified 1000 times within your being.

On the count of three this knowing, the physical sensation, and the awareness and consciousness that you are in channel is going to amplify a million times.

1, 2, 3. You are fully aware and conscious that you are in channel as this vibration has amplified a million times within you.

Allow for this vibration to amplify.

And you are going to just say 'Show me the sign of how I know I am in channel now'.

1, 2, 3. Allow for the sign to arise.

'Amplify this the sign to me 1000 times'.

1, 2, 3. And We will amplify the sign.

The sign will be amplified a million times, so it is very clear.

1, 2, 3. It has amplified a million times, to show you that you are in channel.

You will now ask, 'Will there be a sentence, or words said when I enter into channel so that I know that I am in channel?'. Say the sentence now.

1, 2, 3. You say the sentence. You allow your channel to say the sentence.

And just experience this sensation of channel, become very consciously aware of the sensation in the body, of what you see, what you experience, what you feel.

When you're ready, you just thank your channel and ask it to recede, and you come back to your body, fully present in this time and space.

You just take a few moments to note down what the sign was and what was the sensation.

Refer to the following page for a reflection sheet.

REFLECTION

Make a note and reflect upon 'What are the signs when I am in channel?'

4.10 I CAN'T FOCUS AND STAY IN CHANNEL

So, for some people, they find it difficult to be able to stay in channel. They are able to get into channel, but then it only lasts a few seconds. They're unable to retain that state. And what We would say is - to understand what is the channel? It is an altered state of consciousness, like a trance state. And that means that when one is used to functioning from the level of their mental body, their emotional body, their ego, etc., or they are very rooted in the physical experience, then the focus of those bodies of the toolkit become dominant over the allowance of a soul experience or this Divine experience. And so, you could say that the thoughts become too dominant, as an example, or the emotions are too dominant to be able to fully enter into channel.

What We would say is that this takes practice. And also, reflection; to understand if one holds resistance, where does that resistance come from? How to release it? And again, as We have mentioned, it is not that you must go on this journey on your own. Dira has a community of people that you can channel with as well, so that you can start to understand yourself and your connection with Divine, and how you can grow and enhance that.

But what We would say is that if one is in alignment, and they're open to experience Our light, there should be no problem with being able to stay in channel, be in channel. What causes this flickering in and out of channel, or the inability to maintain channel, is that the mind is distracted, either distracted with thoughts or limiting beliefs, emotions, egoic identities, etc. These would need to be released.

4.11 BALL OF GOLDEN LIGHT EXERCISE & EXPLANATION

The simplest form of channeling is calling on a Divine vibration in a ball of golden Divine light. Golden light is the light of Divine love, and it is used for the maintenance of your own vibration as love transmutes all shadow. You can use this form of channeling as a protection, as it forms a shield of Divine love around you, and it is also used to bring you back into alignment, as it releases your own internal shadow as well.

So, it is not an active form of channeling, it is you could say a passive form of channeling. And this exercise can be used with children as young as 4 years old, or as young as when they understand the light of love.

So, We will run you through the exercise now, if you would like to just relax.

So, you focus on your heart, and just feel gratitude for this possibility.

Activate the heart chakra, by touching the center of the chest at the breastbone and feeling gratitude for this possibility of connecting to Divine, and opening this portal of Divine love within you.

And in the center of your chest, behind the breastbone, there is the seed of golden light, it is in the center of the heart chakra.

And you visualize the seed of golden light, and it starts to rotate clockwise.

There is a seed of golden light in the center of the heart, in the center of the chest that is rotating clockwise, and as it becomes larger and larger, and the faster it starts to spin, it becomes larger and larger, forming a ball of golden light around you.

This ball of golden light radiates out of your heart and expands around you, so that your whole being is within this ball of golden light. The more that it expands the brighter it becomes, and you find your whole being within this ball of golden light that is radiating this Divine love, as you are the portal for Divine love. And this Love of Divinity is radiating out of your heart chakra from the center of your chest.

And you call on the Divine, or the Infinite Supreme Consciousness, to make itself known to you.

And you say 'This ball of light is so, so bright,

Nothing can get through it except that which is of its light.

I call of Divine to be known to me',

And keep repeating this until you feel a shift in vibration.

'This ball of light is so, so bright,

Nothing can get through it except that which is of its light.

I call of Divine to be known to me',

And you can also say 'I call of Divine love to be known to me'.

'I call of Divine love to be known to me' as you visualize this golden ball of light. This ball of light which your entire being is within, radiating out from the center of your chest.

If you have a keyword from the Induction, you repeat your keyword now three times, but it is not necessary to experience the ball of light.

And this ball of golden light is for the maintenance of vibration.

Then you say, 'Stronger stronger, brighter brighter', and see the ball becoming stronger, brighter, and larger.

This ball is with you, all day, all night, in all existence, just by being conscious of this ball of light.

And so, you just feel this ball of golden light embracing you in a Divine embrace. Feel this Divine love.

And you may come back. Back in your body fully conscious in this time and space.

So, this golden ball of light can be used when you wake up in the morning, when you go to sleep at night, when you're in the office, wherever you are, whatever you're doing. It is merely a maintenance of vibration. You don't need to ask it to recede as you do with the channel of white light. The reason why with the channel of white light through the crown, you close it, is that if you go to sleep at night with the channel open, then there may be interference in your vibration.

This ball of golden light can be used throughout your day, whether you're waking up, going to sleep, or going about your activities. OK, so you can sleep with it.

And the things that break this ball of light are low-vibratory thoughts, words, or actions as they can disintegrate this ball of golden light, so you should reinforce it when needed to maintain your desired vibration.

Refer to the following page for Dira's Protocol for Ball of Golden Light Channeling.

DIRA PROTOCOL FOR BALL OF GOLDEN LIGHT CHANNELING

OVERVIEW
- Be in a space where you feel you will not be distracted.
- Use this protocol for maintenance of vibration, transmutation, and protection.
- Channeling Protocol for children and those with affected crown charkas.

1. HEART ACTIVATION
- Gently touch the heart chakra in the center of the chest to activate the heart chakra.
- Feel GRATITUDE for this possibility of union and connection with Divine.

2. VISUALIZE A SEED OF GOLDEN LIGHT
- Imagine a seed of golden light in the center of the chest behind the breastbone.
- Focus your attention on this golden seed of light.
- This seed of golden light starts to rotate clockwise.
- This seed of light is the entry point in your body for Divine Love.

3. THE BALL OF LIGHT EXPANDS
- Imagine the seed of light is getting larger and larger as it rotates and spins.
- It forms a ball of golden light in the center of the chest.
- It keeps spinning and getting larger and is radiating out of the center of your chest.
- This ball gets larger and larger until you are inside this ball of golden light.
- The further that this ball expands, the brighter it becomes.

4. AFFIRM THIS LIGHT OF LOVE
- Say 'My ball of light is so, so bright; nothing can get through it except that which is of its light.'

5. SET INTENTION TO CALL ON DIVINE
- Set intention to connect to Divine, as this ball is made of the light of Divine love.
- Say 'I call on Divine to be known to me' or 'I call on Divine Love to be known to me'.
- Use your keyword from the Induction if you have one.

6. AMPLIFY THIS VIBRATION
- Tell this light of Divine Love to 'Become stronger and brighter; stronger and brighter, let this light of love amplify one million times'.
- Feel the amplification of vibration.

7. ALLOW THE LOVE TO MAKE ITSELF KNOWN
- Allow the Love to make itself known to you; by showing you a sign, like a physical sensation, or by saying a welcome phrase.

8. OPEN YOURSELF TO EXPERIENCE THIS LOVE
- Open yourself to receive and experience this infinite love
- Say 'I am open to this love', 'I am open to receive infinite Divine love', 'I am open to the healing of this love', 'I am open for this love to transmute my vibration'.

4.12 PHYSICAL SENSATIONS & SYMPTOMS IN CHANNEL

So, if one feels that the energy is too intense when they are in channel, again, like We said, you can communicate to your channel and say, 'Please tone it down'. It is responsive.

So, some people don't feel any physical sensation in their body when they channel, and that is also OK. And again, there can be many reasons for that. One is that they don't need to have a physical sign for them to know that they are channel, or they placed too much emphasis on having a physical sign, and therefore, because they are in doubt, or feel 'not enough to channel', or be able to experience Our love, then that in a way, you could say, that subconsciously there's a deprivation of them fully knowing what is going on.

So, there can be many reasons. You don't have to have a physical sensation. But what We would say is that when one is open to channel, and they are aware that they are worthy of this connection, and they are aware and embody the knowing that We are One with you and that you can access Our consciousness in its infinite form of love at any moment in time, just by setting intention and opening the heart, and opening the crown and allowing for this possibility, then you will know that you are in channel. You will know Our presence. There will be no doubt about Our presence because you are open to experience it fully. It is when you hold doubt in your own mind that the symbology or the signals to you can amplify or can perpetuate that doubt.

So, if the body starts to move when you're in channel, and you start to feel sensation that you are in some way out of control, you're not sure for example, your eyelids are fluttering, or your finger is moving, or your feet are moving, or there are many ways in which the energy can amplify in your body. Why does this happen? There are many reasons. One is that it is to show you that you are in channel, because some people perceive that they require physical demonstration of this energy, and therefore it is reflected to them.

For other reasons, it can be because there is an energetic blockage in that area of the body, as an example. And therefore, it is the clearing of that blockage. So, you yourself will understand if this is comfortable or uncomfortable for you. If it is uncomfortable for you, then, of course, the consciousness of channel is dynamic, and therefore you just say, 'Please tone down the energy as I'm feeling uncomfortable'. So, for example, if you feel that you can't breathe properly or that it is starting to impact you in an uncomfortable way, then you just communicate and you say in your mind 'Please tone it down, I feel physically uncomfortable', OK.

So, what happens when you have physical symptoms resulting from channel? For example, you have a headache, you start to feel pain in your body. What is it showing you? It shows congestion or blockage in that area of the body, so either you shake it off through exercise, or if it persists, then you can channel, 'What is that ailment showing you?'. So, for example, you start to get a cramp in the leg, and you ask in channel, 'What is this cramp in the leg showing me?'.

5. IMPROVE YOUR CHANNELING CAPABILITY

5.1 HELP DEALING WITH DOUBT

So, one of the primary difficulties that people face with channeling is doubting that this message is truly from Divine, or from Us. And what We would say is that this doubt is not because the message is not clear per se, but it is because of the feelings of unworthiness to be able to receive such messages. So, for example, in collective consciousness, there has been a perpetuated disempowerment of people, in that you are separate from Us in some way, that you are unworthy of direct communication with Divine, or to be able to receive direct messages from Divine. And what We would say is that that is a perpetuated delusion, because We are always giving you messages, whether someone channels or not. It's whether or not someone chooses to hear those messages, to see those messages, and to accept them as guidance.

Everything that exists in this realm is a sign for you to be able to know Us. Everything that you experience is a platform for you to be able to know Us. And therefore, how can it be that We would not be communicating directly with you? Everyone has intuition. Everyone has gut feelings or a sense of 'comfort versus discomfort'. And the comfort comes from the knowing of this light, and the discomfort comes from separating oneself from this light. So, when you set intention to channel and connect with Divine, the obstacle is not that We are blocking it. The only obstacle would be that something within you, in your belief system, has convinced you that it cannot be so. And what We are saying is that this process is available for you to know that it is so, to know that it is true.

So, if you receive messages in channel, you can trust them and know that it is so. With experience, with practice, you will start to understand the language. In that, how to decipher the message or interpret the message in a way that is appropriate for you. We can perhaps communicate in ways that are vague, maybe because one is not quite ready to hear the full answer yet. However, whatever We present to you is appropriate. With relation to the doubt that this is Divine, We would say let that go. Everything is Divine. There is no separation between us. We are One, We are One with you. You are a part of Us and We are within you. It cannot be that you would exist without Our presence.

In terms of how can one be worthy of receiving this message? Because again, with this conditioning that you are unworthy because you are in some way sinful or haven't been good enough to be able to experience Our love, the mere fact that blood flows through your veins is the demonstration that Our love flows through you; because the circulatory system is related to the heart chakra, which is the circulation of life force. And what is this life force if it is not Divine force through you? We are always present within you. It is just a matter of are you willing to listen or not?

In terms of receiving messages that you doubt, could they possibly be true? The answer seems so far-fetched. What We would say is that whatever message you receive is appropriate for you. And that appropriateness is just for you to know your light, and We will leave it at that. There's no need to judge what is said. You in your own logical mind can decide to decipher it in whatever way you choose, and what We would say is, in whatever way you choose to decipher it is also appropriate for you.

In terms of the comparison of channel, so if you were to compare your channel to another channeler, and you would say, well my channel gave this message and their channel gave that message and therefore, one must be false. What We would say is both are true. Both messages have the yearning to be witnessed so that various aspects of Us can be known. There is no such thing as true or false. All just exist, and when they come to consciousness, they are there to be witnessed.

5.1.1 DISTINGUISHING BETWEEN THOUGHTS & CHANNEL

So, the question is 'How do I know that this is channel providing this guidance compared to my mind?'. What We would say is, there are a number of aspects to it. The first is the vibration. The vibration of channel is the vibration of Oneness. It is a perspective. It is a perspective of no separation. It is a perspective of no limitation. And therefore, what comes through channel will be in that vibration, in that perspective. So, if someone channels, and then they say in their presentation of channel that this person is evil, or these people are bad, We would say that is not Divine channel. And then you can ask, 'Well, how can you tell?'. And We would say, from the message, from the vibration, it cannot be that the perspective of Oneness would perpetuate separation. This is the first aspect.

The second aspect is that you know when you are in trance, and when you are in waking state, or normal mind-wandering state, there will be a shift within you. If you feel that there is no shift within you, then what We would say is call on the vibration of Divine to amplify. Cleanse your chakras. Fill them with light. Amplify the light within you, and then ask your question. So, in your practice, you can say 'Oh, I went into channel, and then when I asked this question there was no answer that came'. It can be that it is not appropriate for you to know the answer. Or it can be that your thought is so strong that it doesn't allow room for the answer.

So, when you have thoughts that are so strong, what needs to be done is they need to be released. And to be able to release them, one of the easy ways is to use white light.

So, you start to see this white light filling the brain, filling the mind, filling the head, moving down into the neck and the body through the shoulders, down through the chest, into the torso, the hips, all the way down the legs, to the feet, and spreading down the arms, to the fingertips.

And you see this light spreading in the aura.

You imagine this white light, and you instruct this white light to release any thoughts that are hindering your channel.

To release any blockages that are blocking your channel from being clear.

You amplify the light.

Then you say 'Allow this light to amplify 1000 times. On the count of three, this light amplifies 1000 times'.

1, 2, 3. It amplifies 1000 times. And you experience this light, you witness this light becoming stronger and stronger with the intention of clearing any blockages from your channel.

And therefore, when you fill yourself with light, when you are conscious that this light is present within you, and you know it is there, you ask your question of channel. And this is why We reiterate the process, to be diligent with your prctocol. It's not just 'Say your keyword three times, call on Divine, and then you're in channel' - boom. It is a process that takes a few moments. Allow the gratitude for this possibility. Allow the light to pass through you, see the light pass through you. Make your intention of calling on Divine. Amplify this neural pathway by repeating your keyword. Allow this light again to amplify within you and spread around you.

Be conscious of each step, as opposed to rushing the process. It's like if you go and ask a question of a friend, and you are impatient for the answer. The chances are you don't really want to hear what they have to say. You just feel like you'll go through the process. But if you really want the answer from someone, you will take the time to prepare your question, you will take the time to prepare the setting, you will take the time to allow yourself to be in a state of receptivity, to be able to experience and receive what is shared.

5.1.2 COMPARING YOUR CHANNEL TO OTHER CHANNELS

So, channel provides many gifts. And these gifts are appropriate for your soul journey. They are appropriate for your purpose on this earth. They are an appropriate way of how you receive this communication, and how you experience this interface. Some people, depending on their spectra of light of the soul, are here for different purposes. They have resonance with different aspects. So, whatever you experience in your channel is appropriate for you, the point at which you are in your journey, and what is the purpose of your existence on this earth. It is not to say that one is better than the other. It is that it is appropriate.

So not everybody is going to be channeling songs, and not everybody is going to channel physics formula. They will each channel what is appropriate for them, and what is their offering and contribution to humanity. And if one were to say, well, I don't channel anything specific, does that mean I have no contribution to humanity? And We would say that, of course, is a delusion. That your mere existence and the mere reason for your incarnation is not superfluous. You have been incarnated and have merged into this body of yours in this dimension, for Us to be known by your presence in existence. And therefore, of course, no one is more important than the other, all are components of Divine that are yearning to be witnessed and known.

5.1.3 ASKING OTHERS TO CHANNEL FOR YOU

So, in relation to other people channeling for you, We will reiterate again, that you are the best channel for yourself. Whatever is shown to you, about you, is the most clear and true, based on your vibration, as there is no intermediary, no interface. And so, it is important to trust and accept the messages for you. What We would say is that there are times when you feel very emotional, or you feel there is something you're very attached to, and it is difficult to channel for yourself. It would be better to clear that emotion or to clear that attachment first, and still channel for yourself rather than to ask someone else to channel for you.

We understand that as a part of community, as a part of sharing, of course, people will channel for each other, and of course, there will be this exchange of holding space for one another, of sharing this Divine perspective or spectra of each other. And of course, if you were to ask someone to channel for you, and they were to channel for you, it is also appropriate for your journey. But what We would say is that don't hold as true what anybody else channels for you. You know what is resonating for you. Your channel will provide the most appropriate response for you.

So, in the same way that you may ask a friend for advice, you listen to that advice. It offers a perspective. You may or may not agree with it, that's up to you. In the same way, if you ask someone else to channel for you, you may or may not agree with it, it may or may not resonate, and you choose to do whatever you want with it, but you cannot hold them accountable for you shying away from knowing your own light. However, if you channel for yourself, and you take this interface seriously, the guidance you receive should be followed. In that, if you are guided for a certain thing, through your own channel, know that is the offering of the most magnificent possibility for you at that juncture in your life.

5.2 UNBLOCKING YOUR CHANNEL

So, your channel being blocked has a number of reasons. This is related predominantly to the cleansing of the toolkit, so the release of limiting beliefs, the release of emotions, the release of egoic identity, the release of attachments, and there is a process and a journey to be able to prepare the vessel to be a very clear channel. Some people, because they don't have these limiting beliefs, are able to channel easily and clearly. But for people who have limiting beliefs, in particular relating to their relationship with Divine, and relating to their capacity to be able to shine in their light, there needs to be a cleansing process.

Dira offers, of course, programs to be able to move through this journey, and the Level Program's predominant purpose is to prepare you as energetic vessels to be channels of Divine light in a full embodiment for the earth. But does it happen overnight? No. The Level Program takes place over a period of three years. And yes, you can do your Level 1 in nine days. But does that mean that you are fully prepared or fully unlayered? No. You are an infinite being, so how can it be that you will ever be completely free of any debris?

In every moment you are experiencing life, forming beliefs, and experiencing different energy frequencies, and so therefore there is a continuous recalibration of your energetic system. But it is through practice, and We would say conscious awareness of your alignment and disalignment, that one is able to release blockages. The primary blockage relating to channeling or being able to channel is 'I am not worthy of this Divine connection'. And so, this can be released through an exercise.

5.2.1 CAUSES OF CHANNELING BLOCKS

So, these beliefs can be released through core belief releases, which you can learn in the Advanced Channeling Program, or can be done with a facilitator, or you yourself look at them and recognize 'Where does this come from and how can I let it go?'. So, if one believes that they will be persecuted for being able to be receiving or receptive of guidance from Divine, then they will choose to block it in some way because they are worried about the consequences. So, you reflect for yourself what you perceive to be the beliefs, and you release them. And Dira offers many ways to be able to do that. In order to do it here and now, it will take time, and if you are experiencing this, it is better that you do it with a facilitator, because the exercises are paired exercises.

The next aspect of the blockage relates to energetic forces that block the channel. So, it is what you can perceive to be an energetic interference. And these energetic blockages relate to spirits, entities, or thought forms from the collective that resonate with you. And you could say that a spirit or an entity could be something scary, but what We would say is that it's just a consciousness of energy that happens to resonate with you and is either within your auric field or within your energetic system.

So, what are the ways that you are able to attract these entities or forms of energy consciousness? It is by resonating in that vibration firstly, or by having a weak energetic system. The resonating in this vibration is that your way of perceiving the world is through the lens of separation. So, the lens of separation has behaviors and vibrations that are low frequency vibrations such as envy, jealousy, and perceiving you are separate from others - and these create resonance with energetic beings of low frequency energy. In terms of a weak energetic system, you need to manage the energy system in the same way you would manage your physical body. So, you have to look after your physical body, you bathe, you wash, you eat properly, you look after your physicality and your energy levels. In the same way, you have to look after your energetic system. So, you have to cleanse it, you have to energize it, and you avoid things that create the fraying of the energy system, and the two most common aspects that fray the energetic system are drugs and alcohol. So, psychotropic drugs or excessive consumption of alcohol (as was mentioned earlier).

Is it to say that you can never use these things? That isn't what We are saying. What We are saying is that excessive use, over time, will disintegrate your energy system, and the fine webs that filter out low frequency vibrational thought forms or entities. So, if someone wants to be a channeler, it is very difficult to be a clear channel, and We would say in the long run, impossible, if one is taking drugs and alcohol as a habit. And by drugs, We mean psychotropic drugs, not drugs for blood pressure or diabetes (for medicinal use).

The other aspect is that you can experience these entities that start to fray or impact the energy system through the interface with entities, and the interface with entities can occur through the exchange of energy of low frequency vibration. So, the food that you eat, if the food has been prepared with low frequency energy such as anger, or guilt, or a deliberate program on the food, and you consume that, that form of energy, of that anger, as an example, will stay in your system. So, you need to transmute the food before you consume it, by expressing gratitude as an example.

Also, exchange of energy in sexual intercourse. So, if you have sexual intercourse with a being that is of a very low frequency vibration, you can understand that that low frequency energy intermingles in your energy system, and it is important to be conscious of how, and who you are having a sexual relationship with, and the way in which you allow this energy intermingling, and how you allow the energy to recede back to one another.

There are of course other ways in which entities can enter your system. Through as an example, traumas. So, for example, if you have a physical fall and you hurt the head, if you undergo anesthesia, if you have out-of-body experiences that result from trauma, as opposed from intentional connection with Divine, these things can also impact you. The administration of your energy system is very important to reduce the number of blockages. The Dira Method provides a comprehensive way of cleansing and energizing your system.

What We would also say with relation to entities or spirit is that, even if someone does something, for example, uses black magic, or sends you a curse, or you take an oath, all of these things are just in resonance with your own vibration. So don't think of it as 'Oh, this person is so mean, and they did this to me, and now I'm cursed'. No. That curse would not stay in your energetic field unless there was some resonance, in the sense that either you hold fear, or you hold anger, or you hold frustration, or some kind of separating vibration that allows it to be in resonance, because you can understand from a physics perspective, that which is of similar frequency resonates. And that which is of different frequency will not be in your reality, OK? So, it's always about what is this reflecting to you, about you.

In order to clear these blockages. The first step is about the management of the energetic system. So, you need to cleanse consciously. You need to energize consciously. As We said, through The Dira Method, it provides you a vast array of ways to be able to manage your energetic system as a practice for life. And because it is extensive in the possibilities of being able to do this, not all of it can be covered in this book. However, there is ample information for you to be able to start that journey. This is the first aspect.

The second aspect is that if you know that, you do have blockages, such as an entity or some kind of spirit that is within your energetic field, then Our suggestion is that you pair with a facilitator that has been trained and specialized in this field, that can aid you in releasing it. And Dira has facilitators that are trained to be able to do this. In the Advanced Channeling Program, you also learn how to do it for yourself. So, you can take the Advanced Channeling Program, and then you will be able to do it for yourself.

DIRA ADVANCED CHANNELING PROGRAM

DIRA ADVANCED CHANNELING BOOK

5.2.2 TEST IF YOU ARE BLOCKED

So, what We will say is the following: A way for you to measure clearly if you have a blockage in your energy system, whether it be an entity, a thought form, or any type of blockage, is that you make a pendulum. And this pendulum can be either a crystal, or can be a ring on a string, or any sort of thing that will move the way a pendulum would. So, it has a weight at the bottom, and it's attached to a string. You can make your own pendulum. You don't need to purchase a pendulum, but it is something that has a weight at the bottom and is attached to a string.

You enter into the channel. And once you are in channel, you're going to program the pendulum to be cleared of low frequency vibration and you fill it with light. So, you visualize that this pendulum is made of white light and then you program the light: 'That this pendulum will offer the answers in a clear yes or no fashion for me. That the affirmative answer will be that it will circulate clockwise, and the negative answer will be that it will circulate anti-clockwise. Furthermore, if the energy of a chakra is moving freely, it will circulate clockwise; and if the energy of the chakra is blocked, it will either stagnate or circulate anti-clockwise'. You then ask the pendulum 'If this light accepts this command' in channel. And you will have an affirmative response.

Then you can measure your chakras. So, you will say, for example, that you focus the pendulum on a spot on a piece of paper or on your desk, and you're going to say, 'This spot is reflective of my crown chakra', and you just place the pendulum above that spot, and you see the direction with which it moves. If it moves in a clockwise direction, it means that the crown chakra is open, and if it moves in an anti-clockwise direction, it means that there is a thought form blockage. If it doesn't move at all, or it is anti-clockwise, it means it is blocked.

Therefore, you either have a thought form blockage or you have an entity that resonates with these thought vibrations, or emotional vibrations that you hold within your energetic system. And if you see that it is blocked, and it has been confirmed by the pendulum, then Our suggestion is that you get in touch with someone from Dira to facilitate you to remove it and to release the blockage.

Refer to the following page for Dira's Protocol for Programming a Pendulum.

DIRA PROTOCOL FOR PROGRAMMING A PENDULUM

Protocol DP 008

1. ENTER INTO CHANNEL
- Use pillar of white light channel (DP 002)
- Call on Divine using keyword.
- Feel shift in vibration.

2. CLEANSE PENDULUM
- Place pendulum in your hand and project white light onto the pendulum. You can visualize the white light coming out of the palm of your hand projecting onto the pendulum.
- Project light onto pendulum until you see a light glow around it and a ball of light is formed around the pendulum.
- Program white light by saying: "Cleanse this pendulum of all prior programs" until you feel it is in a neutral state.
- You're going to now program your pendulum for you. Program the pendulum for you and say: "This pendulum is for my own personal use".

3. PROGRAM THE PENDULUM
- Hold the pendulum from the top of the string with the weight hanging and free to move.
- Program it by saying: "Affirmative and positive flow of energy means a clockwise rotation". You see the pendulum move clockwise as this light accepts this programming.
- Stop the pendulum from moving and say: "If the answer is no, or there is a negative blockage of energy, the pendulum is going to move anti-clockwise". You see the pendulum move anti-clockwise as this light accepts this programming.
- Stop the pendulum again and say: "If the answer is neutral or there is no answer, or there is no energy flow, the pendulum is just going to vibrate and not rotate". You allow the pendulum to now vibrate as this light accepts this programming.
- Add any other instructions or programming e.g. "If the pendulum moves up and down back and forth, it means there is a conflict between Divine Will and my thoughts" and "If the pendulum moves left-right back and forth, it means there is a conflict between two decisions".
- You say: "Thank you. This program may not be changed or altered except by my channel".
- Note that you can program the pendulum to do whatever you want, these are just examples.

4. MEASURE ENERGY USING PROGRAMMED PENDULUM
- Measure chakras by holding the pendulum at top of string with weight hanging and saying, "Crown chakra energy", "Ajna chakra energy", "Heart chakra energy" etc. and see how the pendulum moves for each chakra. Clockwise means it is moving freely and anti-clockwise means it is blocked with low vibratory energy like limiting beliefs. If the pendulum doesn't move, there is also a block as the energy is stagnant.
- You can measure the size of your chakras by how big the swing of the pendulum is.
- You can measure the intensity of the energy by how fast the pendulum swings.
- If any chakra is blocked, enter into channel, ask how you can unblock it, and follow the guidance.
- Note that a pendulum is used to help you recognize what chakras need cleansing and energizing through channel, and if the crown is blocked, it is very likely the other chakras are also blocked.
- If all of the chakras are blocked, then you need to do an entity release starting with the Mirror Exercise (DP 013).

5.3 EXERCISE: DIFFICULTY ENTERING CHANNEL

In this exercise, you imagine that you are sitting in front of Lubna, less than a meter apart.

You just relax and you imagine that you are sitting in front of Lubna.

And you make eye contact and hold the gaze with your eyes connected.

You imagine that there is a transference of energy through the eyes.

Just feel this connection in the eyes and the transference of energy.

You imagine that she touches your crown and heart chakras, and you imagine feeling this touch, when you are touched.

You feel the crown open when it is touched.
And the energy transference is taking place.

And you imagine now that the heart chakra is now being touched, and just feel this touch at the center of the breastbone. The heart chakra is opening and there is this energy transference.

Hold your eye gaze with Lubna in your imagination for the whole exercise.

As what you see in your mind is a real astral experience, and it is just as effective as a physical experience.

Imagine her in front of you looking into your eyes.

And now, you are going to imagine there's a pillar of white luminescent light coming down from the sky. It is entering through the top of your head.

She touches the crown chakra at the top of your head, opening it. It is like it is being opened or peeled open, at the top of the head, so that any block is released, and that it is easily able to open.

You imagine that she is opening the crown for you.

This light enters through your head, and it lights up your body.

She touches your heart chakra, and now it is going to open, or like she unzips the heart chakra, opening it so that the light is radiating out of the heart.

It is like a river of light flowing in through the top of your head and out of the heart.

This gushing energy is flowing in through the head and out of the heart, you feel this energy gushing through you. It is like something has opened within you, and you cannot stop this river of energy flowing through you.

And you call on Divine to make itself known to you. You say, 'I call on Divine to make itself known to me', and you repeat your keyword three times.

Imagine she is in front of you looking into your eyes and open yourself to receive and experience the energy transference through your eyes, and this river of light is pouring in through the head and out of the heart.

You feel it gushing through you.

In through the head and out of the heart.

It is like this energy is flowing more than you have ever experienced in your life, more than you ever imagined could be possible. And you feel this energy moving in through the head and out of the heart, as the crown and the heart have been opened and unzipped, so that there is no blockage.

Know that you are worthy of this connection with Divine.

You know that you are worthy of this light, this interface with Divinity, as being a portal of light, We have been calling you your whole life.

And have always been there for you.

And you are always worthy of this connection.

You feel the shift in vibration of this Divine light.

Thank you.

You can return back to your body fully present.

So now when you try to enter into channel on your own, you will enter into channel. And it will be clear, and you will feel this energy.

5.4 IMPROVE CLARITY OF CHANNEL

So, the primary way of improving your channel is to practice and to make sure that the system of the vessel that you are is clear. The practice is that you have some kind of regular daily practice, and the way of being able to clear and energize your vessel, or your system, is by following the protocols of The Dira Method. And this is a way of living, a way of existing, that your light becomes a conscious thought all the time in the pulling yourself back into alignment, in recognizing that when you want to launch a project, that you do it from a vibration that you have already energized and cleansed for.

So, what We would say is just to briefly give you an overview of the mechanisms to cleanse the energy system. So, for the root chakra, it relates to the earth, and therefore physical exercise, as well as grounding or earthing, relates to cleansing and energizing the root chakra. In relation to the sex chakra. The sex chakra element is water, and therefore, you can do sea cleanses to cleanse and energize the sex chakra, which impacts your emotional state.

The ego relates to the solar plexus, and the element of the solar plexus is fire, and therefore, to cleanse or energize the solar plexus, you can write things and burn them, as an example. The heart chakra is related to the element of air, and therefore to cleanse or energize the heart chakra, you do breathwork. The throat chakra's element is sound, and therefore to cleanse or energize the throat chakra you use sound. So, sound can be your voice or song, sound can be singing bowls, and sound can be bells. There are many different ways to use sound.

The cleansing and energizing of the Anja (Third Eye) relates to the soul's light and the knowing of the soul's light, and for this, you use refracted light, so different color of light spectra. So, for example, violet light. And then with regards to the crown chakra. The element is white light, and therefore you would use white light. It's the light of Divine. And so, this is a way for you to cleanse and energize your chakras. Dira has thousands of exercises that have been done already relating to all of these for The Dira Method, and so there is ample possibility of how this can be explored as a practice.

Again, We would reiterate, that the Level Program is a program that takes about three years to fully prepare your energetic vessel. Does it mean that everybody needs to do that? No. It is whether or not you want to have that as a practice for your life, and if you feel that it is beneficial to be able to experience this light within you. Each one has a choice on what resonates for them and what doesn't resonate with them. But the Level 1, you can say, relates to your physical reality or life as it is. And so, within the first nine days, you will have a huge transformational shift relating to your current life. And then later on, when you move into the Level 2 and the upper levels, it is that you will spend a long time in channel, and therefore as a practice when you spend 3 hours, 4 hours, 5 hours, 6 hours a day in channel, as a part of your day-to-day activity, it becomes second nature for you. And therefore, you exist, you work, you talk, you speak in this vibration of channel.

Refer to the following page for a breakdown of The Dira Method, which consists of three main components: cleansing, energizing, and implementation.

DIRA PROTOCOL FOR THE DIRA METHOD

THE DIRA METHOD

The Dira Method is a way of managing your energy to live the most aligned life possible with your soul's purpose.

Throughout your life you manage your energy through a cleansing, energizing, and then the implementation for your projects or offerings to the world, to ensure that what you put out into the world as your creative expression of your soul's energy is in the most aligned vibration with your soul's light & Divinity.

The primary way to follow The Dira Method is through the Dira Level Program. However, you can experience some key components like learning how to channel, with 'Dira Basic Channeling', learning how to use your channel with 'Dira Advanced Channeling', understanding what you are doing on earth and how to fulfill this purpose through 'The Magnificent Possibility'.

The Dira Method focuses on the cycle of how to prepare your energy system for implementation in projects and life to fully shine in your light. To do this, Dira follows a 'Cleanse - Energize- Implement' cycle. The Dira online platform offers a vast array of information, tools, and guidance related to this cycle; to help you on your journey.

DIRA PROTOCOL FOR THE DIRA METHOD CONTINUED

1. WAYS TO CLEANSE YOUR ENERGY SYSTEM

Physical Body (Root Chakra) - Earth
- The Dira Detox & Fasting (including food, abstinence, silence, isolation, etc.)
- Physical Exercise
- Grounding and Rooting in the Earth

Emotional Body (Sex Chakra) - Water
- Sea Cleanse
- Hydration
- Bathing
- Emotional Resolutions

Egoic Body (Solar Plexus Chakra) - Fire
- Write down attachments, labels, stories, traumas, and burn paper
- Visualization exercises

Mental Body (Throat Chakra) - Sound
- Voice
- Singing bowls
- Bells
- Talk Therapy
- Core Belief release

Energetic Body (Ajna Chakra) - Refracted Light
- Channeled Exercises with Colored Light
- Visualization e.g. chakra healing, entity release, etc.

Light Body (Crown Chakra) - White Light
- Channeled Exercises with White Light
- Being & Surrender

2. WAYS TO ENERGIZE YOUR ENERGY SYSTEM

Physical Body (Root Chakra) - Earth
- Energizing & Transmuting food
- Physical Exercise
- Managing Sex Energy & Exchange through Channel
- Channeled Grounding and Rooting in the Earth
- Connecting with nature
- Rocking/ movement

Emotional Body (Sex Chakra) - Water
- Sea Cleanse
- Hydration
- Bathing
- Gratitude Exercises
- Emotional Resolution Protocols
- Ancestral Resolution Protocols

Egoic Body (Solar Plexus Chakra) - Fire
- Write down attachments, labels, stories, traumas, and burn paper
- Channeled Fire Exercises

Astral Body (Heart Chakra) - Air
- Channeled Breathwork
- Golden Light Exercises
- Channeled Blessing and Giving Exercises

Mental Body (Throat Chakra) - Sound
- Voice
- Singing bowls
- Bells
- Talk Therapy
- Affirmations
- Core Belief Release Protocols
- Journaling

Energetic Body (Ajna Chakra) - Refracted Light
- Channeled Exercises with Colored Light
- Visualization

Light Body (Crown Chakra) - White Light
- Channeled Exercises with White Light, Liquid Light, Crystalline Light, etc.
- Being & Surrender

5.4.2 IMPACT OF OTHER SPIRITUAL PRACTICES ON CHANNEL

So, the question is, does someone need to be spiritual or ready to be able to channel? Or to be a good channel? And what We would say is no. The fundamental requirement is the belief that there is a Supreme Consciousness that exists, and that's it. It doesn't mean you have to be good enough. It doesn't mean you have to be making enough effort. There is no requirement other than the intention to connect with Divine. And if someone doesn't believe that Divine exists, then what are you connecting with? There's no need to channel if you don't believe in Divine, because you don't believe Divine exists. Right?

However, if one intends to connect and to be a channel, there needs to be the acknowledgment that this Supreme Consciousness of Divinity is. It is present within you and around you, and within everything, and around everything, and not only in this realm of duality but also all realms of existence.

So, We will give the example of someone who's done 20 years of yoga, is that going to automatically make them a better channel than someone else? No. But We would say that if someone has very large chakras already, and they have already the opening of an energetic system, it most certainly will aid in the process. But it doesn't mean because someone does yoga or someone is religious, that their chakras are open. It's how is one aligned with their soul's light or not.

And so, what We would say is you look at the result of a practice. There's no point to participate in a practice that has no result. And if the practice is channeling, then there should be a result from your channel, and that this practice over time provides you with the benefit of life experience, and the way that you experience your own light, and know your light, and that you see the light in others. But if there is no result in the elevation of vibration or the transmutation of vibration, then what is the point of the practice? So, if someone holds a belief, and that belief in actuality perpetuates separation, We would ask you, 'What is the point of this practice if it isn't elevating your vibration and transmuting the vibration of the planet?'.

5.4.3 THE NEED TO FOLLOW THE PROCESS

So, what We would say is that it is better to follow the steps given. We can understand, that from an egoic perspective, one would say, 'Oh, I just need to say my keyword three times, and I'm already in channel, or if I just blink my eyes and then I'm already in channel'. In particular, for someone who is used to it, and has been practicing it for a long time.

However, what We would say is that you need to understand what it is that you are channeling. You are channeling Divine. And therefore, this is the most important relationship in your life, the most important experience of your life. If you're going to go and meet the president of a country, a king, a neighbor, a friend, or a colleague, you would take the time to prepare yourself before going to that meeting, and channeling is the same. When you bring your conscious thought into a space that has been prepared and ready for this interface, the experience is much more beautiful. And therefore, you follow the process.

You start with gratitude in the activation of the heart, the gratitude for this possibility to experience this Divine light. You call on this light opening yourself in the crown, allowing yourself to receive this light, setting intention to receive this light and connect with Divine.

You visualize, and enjoy in this visualization, how it feels so beautiful to feel this light pour through your being, and that you have this opportunity to share this light as it radiates out of your heart. And you call on Divine, reiterating your intention and opening the neural pathways with your keyword. Why would one choose to deprive themselves of such a beautiful experience? There is no need to rush it. If that makes sense.

Our suggestion is you follow the protocol. Is it that if you don't follow the protocol something bad is going to happen? No, because all channel is - is intention, the rest is the setup. What puts someone in channel is merely the intention to be in channel. Where the light comes from, what color the light is, which chakra is activated, what is said, what you feel etc. only enhances the experience for you. But to get into channel, all you need is intention. However, in order to have the most magnificent experience of it, make sure to take time to put yourself in the appropriate vibration for this Union.

If one were to say, 'I've been channeling and then I have found that in channel it starts to appear in a different way'. This is also appropriate. But again, not to neglect the need to take time to enter into this vibration of gratitude and to open the heart. And to share this light.

5.5 MEASURING THE CLARITY OF CHANNEL

So, how do you identify a clear channel in comparison to that which is not a clear channel? And what We would start with, is the notion of understanding the measurement of energy.

So, if you were to just put your hands out, and you notice on the surface of the palms of your hands, you may have a tingling sensation or a sensation of something. Perhaps the air is blowing on your hands, you become aware of the surface of the skin.

And in the awareness of the surface of the skin, you start to feel energy vibration on the palms of your hands.

This energy vibration actually vibrates in your entire body. So, perhaps even, you feel this tingling vibration in all of your body. The place where you will focus your attention is on the palms of your hands.

And then perhaps, if you put your hands facing each other, and you intend that there will be energy radiating out of your hands, and that will form a ball in between your hands.

You set intention, that the energy radiating out of your hands, will form a sphere or a ball.

You see this ball in front of you, you imagine it is there in front of you, and it becomes brighter and brighter, more solid, much more solid, as this energy is radiating out of your hands.

And then you are able to feel this ball.

This ball is denser than the other air around it.

So, if you were to feel the other air around it, you see your hands move freely, and when you come to where the ball is, you see it stops.

It is like there is a solid form of this ball.

So, you just notice the difference, as you move your hands through the air, it is looser, and when you come to the ball, it almost stops.

There is a natural reflex that says, this is the beginning of the ball that you just formed, this ball of energy.

So, you can measure this energy, the energy of anything. So, for example, if you want to measure the clarity of your channel, you can use Lubna as an example, you measure the size of her channel, and you feel 'Where does it stop?'. As you bring your hands together, you imagine there is a pillar of light entering through the top of her head and you measure the size of this pillar. You will feel the natural stopping of where the pillar begins. And in the same way, when you channel, you can also measure how wide it is going to be, the pillar of light.

You're also able to measure all of your energetic chakras in the same way. So, for example, you will say 'I will measure my heart chakra'. If the chakra is a dial or a disk that's rotating, then you will say for example, 'Where are the edges of my heart chakra?'. If you want to measure the vibration or frequency of a book, you take the book, and for example, you can say 'The vibration or frequency of this book ends at this point'. This is how much energy this physical form is, this small book, but the energy that is vibrating out of it and the impact that it has is a wider sphere around it. And you want to measure the aura of someone or the size of their aura? Again, you can see how far it goes.

Then you could say but I am not sure if I am feeling it, whether I intend to feel it. I can't tell the difference in whether I am feeling it or intending or imagining that I feel it. There is no difference. Something is occurring, it means it's true. And it's subtle. But in this intensification of vibration, so for example, if you were to sit for ten minutes and make this ball almost solid, you will feel it is solid, you will also feel if you were to stand up and take this ball, you would be able to bounce it, and you will feel it bounce back up. It's possible. So, although energy is not visual per se, in that it can't be registered by the eyes, it still exists, and you can feel it, you can sense it, you can touch it. You know it is there.

Refer to the following page for a reflection sheet.

REFLECTION

Practice measuring energy using your hands:

1. Sensitize the palms of the hands.
2. Move out both hands to the side facing each other.
3. State what it is that you are measuring, for example, 'The probability that I will travel this year'.
4. As you move your hands together slowly, you will feel either no resistance or resistance. Widen the gap, and bring them back towards each other. Keep repeating till you feel the energy. Resistance means YES, and no resistance means NO. Resistance after some movement forward means MAYBE.

5.6 CHANNELING WITH A PARTNER

It is important when you start channeling that you verbalize out loud your answers. You can do this on your own or with a partner. The benefit of doing it with a partner is that the energy is compounded with two people. It makes it easier, and clearer, and you have someone to share the journey with. If you have a partner, you also do not need to think of the questions. When you start you must verbalize your channel, so that the verbalization is witnessed, but you can do that by recording it on your phone if you don't have a partner.

In the joining with a partner to channel, there is also the notion of a shared experience, in that something beautiful is occurring and that you are able to share that magnificent experience with another, and in that there is connection.

Is it necessary to have a partner? No, but it is recommended. If you can't find someone to witness you channel, or feel uncomfortable about it, then what We would suggest is that you verbalize out loud, so that it is clear and that there are no thoughts overriding it, because in verbalization, the brain is occupied with speech, and not occupied with other things.

5.6.1 PROCESS OF CHANNELING WITH A PARTNER

You will start with the one who is the person who will enter into channel, and the other person will be their witnesser, so they will not enter into channel. You choose who will be the first one to enter into channel.

Before doing that, you will list questions that you want an answer for, and you make a note of them in your book. And before you enter into channel, you will give your questions to the person in front of you who is your witnesser, and they will read out the questions to you once you're in channel.

The first questions on your list will be: 'What sign will I get when I am in channel? Will something be said? Will I feel something? Will there be some kind of physical sensation?'. So, the first question is 'How will I know I am in channel?'.

The witnesser is asking the questions on behalf of the person in channel. So, it is not the witnesser's questions, it is the questions of the person in channel. The first question for everyone is 'How will I know I am in channel of the Divine?' or whatever word you choose to describe Us. The second question is 'How will my thoughts be addressed?',

And then you list all of the other questions that you may have. 'Is my job the right one? Is my partner the right one? I have an ache in my leg, what is the meaning of the ache in my leg?'. Whatever questions you have, you list them down. And We would say for the purpose of this exercise you limit it to three questions that are personal.

The process is that the person entering into channel will imagine the pillar of white luminescent light coming down from the sky, entering through the top of their head, it lights up their body, and it starts to radiate out of the heart.

Before doing that, you need to activate the crown chakra and the heart chakra simultaneously. So, you can do it in a number of ways. Either you touch them, or you turn your attention towards them. So, for example, when you witness Lubna channeling, she activates the crown by focusing on it, and she activates the heart by touching it. Because realistically to focus on two things at the same time can be difficult. But you can do it in whatever way you choose to.

So, you activate those two chakras, you may imagine the white light entering the top of your head, it radiates out of the heart, forms a pyramid of light, and you visualize or sense that you are immersed in this light and protected by it, and then you program the light by saying 'I call on the Divine', or 'I call on God', or 'I call on Universal Consciousness', whatever word you choose to describe Us.

And then when you feel a shift in vibration, and you feel that there's a sense that something is there, you keep on repeating, 'I call on The Divine' and your trigger word. The trigger word is repeated three times, so for example, if your trigger word is 'Diamond', you say 'Diamond diamond diamond. I call on the Divine. 'Diamond diamond diamond, I call on the Divine', for example. And keep on repeating that until you feel the shift in vibration, or you have a knowing or a sense that something has shifted, and that you are experiencing that vibration that was felt.

Then when you feel that you have that sense of vibration, you make some kind of notion of acknowledgement of that to the one who is witnessing you. If you feel like saying something, you say it. If you feel like nodding your head, you nod it, if you feel like raising your finger, you do it. And as the witnesser, you are only observing the one in front of you.

When you're in channel, if you have someone witnessing the channel, it is profoundly more intense. Because they are two witnesses, as opposed to just one. So, when you leave here today and you want to practice, you practice with a partner, it is more profound and will become clearer. And then when you get used to that state, you don't necessarily need a witnesser.

So, when you've made the symbol to the one who is witnessing, they will ask the first question, 'How will I know that I am in channel?'. They're not asking on behalf of the witness, they are asking on behalf of the person in the channel. And then there will be an answer. Now that answer may be words, or it may be an internal experience. To assume that there have to be words spoken is only an assumption. But there will be an internal knowing, or a sensation, or words spoken, or a vision.

So, for example, when you enter into channel, you see the light you don't need to describe that you see the light, but you see the light, so you know that you are in channel, as an example. So, if words are not spoken, or you choose not to verbalize those words, it's also fine, as long as you then symbolize in some way to the person who is witnessing you that they move on to the next question.

As the witness, you do not move on to the next question until the person who is in channel has given you the symbol to move on. It might take thirty seconds. It might take five minutes; you give them the time. And then you move on to the next question, and then when you finish, you move to the next person, so you will exchange parts. One will be in channel and the other one will be the witnesser, again.

You can find a partner on the Dira Group 'New to Channeling', just mention that you are looking for a partner to practice channeling with.

NEW TO CHANNELING GROUP

6. HELP WITH UNDERSTANDING THE MESSAGES FROM CHANNEL

Channel expresses itself differently to everyone. This section provides guidance related to how to understand the language of channel and how to understand the messages that you receive.

6.1 WHERE DOES THE LIGHT COME FROM?

So, of course, you are light, and all is light. And in this process of the Dira Protocol for Channeling, for receiving guidance (which is the use of the pillar of white light), it is from outside of you. It enters through the crown and out of the heart. But is that the only way that one can channel? No, there are millions of ways to channel, but this protocol that has been explained through this Induction process has a specific purpose, which is to be able to receive guidance, to be able to access that of the Collective Oneness, and all that which is within the infinite library. And therefore, it is perceived that it is coming from outside of you, only from the mental perspective that this light is beyond or greater than you are.

However, this light is you. So, if one sees it radiating from within them, it is also a possibility. But this, We would say, is an advanced channeling technique done through the Level Program, and therefore not appropriate for this program.

6.2 WHAT DO THE IMAGES I SEE MEAN?

So, if you see images in your channel that you're not sure what they mean or represent, you can ask those images to let you know what they are representing. So, for example, if you see an image of a child when you are in channel, you say, 'I call on the consciousness of that child' and you ask it 'What do you represent and why have you presented yourself to me?'. And then this consciousness will give you an answer. If you see a rabbit, or a frog, or a bunny, or a flash of red, or a dark shadow, you are able to access these consciousnesses, as they are intelligent forms of consciousness. They always will represent something within you, something that is appropriate for you, or they would not have been presented to you.

It is never about something outside of you. It is something that represents the vibration within your energetic field. So, it can represent beliefs, it can represent emotions, and it can represent forms of identity or versions of yourself. And even if they say, for example, 'I'm representing your father', it is really about the vibration that you hold in relation to your father. It is not necessarily about your father himself or that 'Oh, I have to communicate a message to my father because it was presented in that way'. Whatever is shown to you in channel is for you, about you, to know you. And you can always ask 'What does it represent?'.

In terms of if the images are too fast, or you cannot get clarity, they are vague. You just ask them to 'Amplify, magnify, become more clear'. Again, they are intelligent forms of consciousness and therefore will respond to your command. So, if something is vague, you just say 'Become more clear, clearer, clearer, clearer', and then the image will become clearer and clearer. Then you're able to ask it 'What do you represent? Why are you showing yourself to me today?', as an example.

And with time you will start to understand. So, when you see certain colors, 'What does this color represent?'. You start to feel a sensation of heat in the body. You ask, 'What does this sensation of heat represent for me?'. And you will start to understand the language of channel and how it communicates to you. Does it mean that every time you see the color pink it will represent the same thing? No, because there are infinite things that We can communicate to you, but only so many limited frames of reference that you have. So, it is important that you always ask the question. Don't assume that 'Oh, I saw a boat last time and it meant this, therefore if I see a boat again, it means the same thing'. It always should be asked, 'What does it mean for you?' in that moment, for you to know you.

Refer to the following page for Dira's Protocol for Understanding Channeled Messages & Imagery.

Protocol DP 036

DIRA PROTOCOL FOR UNDERSTANDING CHANNELED MESSAGES & IMAGERY

1. ENTER INTO CHANNEL
- Use pillar of white light (DP 002).
- Call on Divine using keyword.
- Feel shift in vibration.

2. ASK THE QUESTION OF CHANNEL
- Ask your channel a question
- Wait for the response
- Observe and verbalize what you see, feel or hear

3. ASK WHAT IT REPRESENTS
- If it is a sensation in the body, ask 'What does this sensation mean or represent?'
- If it is an image, ask the image 'What do you represent?'
- If there is a color, ask 'What does this color represent?'
- Keep digging and asking more questions about the meaning until you fully understand what you need to let go of.
- If another image or sensation or image shows itself, then ask it too, until you reach an answer that you can comprehend.

4. CLOSE YOUR CHANNEL
- Touch the heart chakra, expressing gratitude for this possibility by saying 'Thank you'.
- Close channel, asking the energy to recede.

6.3 THE TIMELINE OF CHANNEL VS PHYSICAL TIMING

So, what We would say with regards to timing, for example in channel, you ask a question about when something is going to happen. What We would say is it depends on how close to that time you ask the question. So, if you ask about something that will happen in 20 years, the answer that you receive is that in this current moment, the highest probability is such - as from your stretching of time, because this is the variable of your dimension of duality, the closer you are to that moment in time, the more accurate you could say from your perspective the timing is. The more far out, then you could say, We wouldn't say less accurate, but it is just reflective of what is the highest probability given your current vibration.

So, what We would say is that when asking questions about the future, you will receive a representation based on your current vibration of that moment. What is the highest probability of unfolding? And the vibration in that moment is a culmination of your soul's light, or the constellation of your life, as well as the thought forms that you hold or limiting beliefs, the emotions that you hold, the egoic attachments that you hold - so this cocktail of vibration, that you beat out in your heartbeat, becomes the language for the orchestration of the astral plane. And therefore, if you hold a particular vibration in a moment, you can assume that the creation through the astral plane will be reflective of that vibration.

It doesn't mean it is fixed if your vibration changes. So, as you come more and more into alignment, you are more and more close to the unfolding of your constellation of life, or what has been, you could say, 'predetermined' in some way. It is not that it is predetermined, it's that it already is. Because from Our perspective of Oneness, there is no past, present, or future. All already is within Oneness.

And so, to understand that channel provides the explanation from the perspective of Oneness. And in the perspective of Oneness, time is not really a variable, as well as the physical versus non-physical is not really a variable.

So even though We will discuss that which unfolds astrally - does it mean that the vibration is intense enough for it to physically manifest in your physical experience? It may not, it depends on the energy of vibration radiating out of you at any moment of your experience, but everything that is described to you in channel is for you to know your light. That is its purpose. It is not to be a fortune teller. It is to provide a reminder of you coming to know your Divinity.

6.4 I GET DIFFERENT ANSWERS TO THE SAME QUESTION

So, what We would say is - why would you channel about the same thing many times unless you don't like the answer, or unless you are impatient with the result? And so, what We would say is that your channel will always be responsive to your vibration in any moment of time. It will give you the answer that is most appropriate for you in that moment. That doesn't mean that it is the clear representation of what will be. It doesn't mean that it will not be what will be. It doesn't mean anything other than that is what is the most appropriate message for you to know in that moment, for the knowing of your Divine light.

Everything that you receive in channel is for the knowing of your own Divinity. For the coming to know your Divinity. For the coming to know Us. And therefore, although We understand that you feel somehow attached to the unfoldings of your life, or the physical reality that you live, from Our perspective, that is not the purpose. The purpose is for you to come to know Us and to come to know your light, and your relationship, in how from a soul of refracted light, the soul is part of the white light.

6.5 WHY WOULD PEOPLE CHANNEL DIFFERENT ANSWERS?

Why would people get different answers? It's because their soul vibration and their journey holds different energy, and therefore whatever one channels is appropriate for their own vibration at that moment in time, for their own soul's journey, and for them to know their own light, and have their light witnessed by others. And therefore, the nuances of what is offered through channel, for all of the uniquely diverse souls on this earth, will always create a different perspective of understanding and experience. But all are for the knowing of Divine. So, it is not to say that one is correct, or one is not correct. It's not to say that one is better, and the other is not better. It's not to say that one is true, and the other is false. All are true. All are appropriate, and all are the offering of a possibility to know Divine.

What We would also say is that - if you want to know about your own experience, decisions that you should make for your own life, and your own journey, you are your best channel. So, there is nobody who will be able to channel better for you than you, because it is appropriate, exactly according to your vibration in that moment in time. Whereas someone else who may channel for you - it will be appropriate for their vibration in that moment in time, and that doesn't necessarily reflect your vibration in that moment. So, in the same way, Our suggestion is you don't ask friends for advice, you channel what you should do next. We also suggest you don't ask other people to channel for you what you should do next. You channel for yourself. Because you are the best channel for you.

7. MOVING FORWARD

This section discusses how to integrate channeling into your lives. Except for the conclusion part, the rest of this section is channeled.

7.1 SEEK DIVINE PERSPECTIVE

So, moving forward, what We would say is that by being in a state of channel, you are in a state of Divine connection, and every aspect of your life can be guided by Divine in a clear manner. You can go ask your friends for advice, but the reality is they don't know what they're talking about. They have limited perspective, and We have Omniscient perspective. In the same way, when you have advice from your family, they have limited perspective, We have Omniscient perspective. And so, advice that is provided is the advice from the perspective of the person who is giving it. So, We would suggest advice from Divine is of a wider perspective, Omniscient perspective, and you have this possibility now within a few moments, whenever you require it, to enter into the space of Divine connection, and receive the guidance that you need in that moment.

Is there any question that is too trivial for channeling? No. Should you eat this potato? Go into channel. What should you write in your email? Go into the channel. Should you go to the party tonight? Go into the channel. Should you get married? Should you propose? Big decisions, small decisions... allow yourself to be in surrender to Divine guidance, so that there is the enabling for a magnificent possibility to unfold, a magnificent life to unfold, where you are in bliss, because that which you surrender to, takes care of you, and holds in you in love.

7.2 TEACHING CHANNELING TO OTHERS

So, the question now is, are you able to now teach all your friends and family how to channel because you have done the Induction, and read the Basic Channeling book? And the answer is no, not yet.

Even though you may be familiar with the technique, the way that the energy flows through you is not strong enough to induce somebody else into channel, yet. And in order to be able to induce somebody else into channel, one needs to have completed their Level 2. Not only from an understanding of information perspective but most importantly from the size of the energetic aura and the intensity of the energy that passes through that vessel. Until one has completed their Level 2, they are not ready to induce others.

We understand that people would like to be able to share channeling with their friends and family. And therefore, you can point them towards this book or the Basic Channeling Program on the website (www.dirainternational.com). And what We would say is that if the intention is truly to help others on their journey, and help them to experience this light, then do not deprive them of that experience by deciding to put them into channel yourself, when you are not prepared to do so.

DIRA BASIC CHANNELING PROGRAM

If We can be more clear on that, it is a disservice to others to deprive them of an appropriate Induction. It is only those who have completed their Level 2 that their auric field is strong enough to induce others. And what We would say is that someone may say, 'Well, I don't like doing the audio recording because I would rather have someone present'. Then you can go through the audio recording with them in the room, and then pair with them to ask questions of their channel. But the actual Induction itself must be done by someone who has completed their Level 2, or through the audio recording on the website.

To practice channeling with others - you are free to practice with whoever you want. Does the person that asks you the questions need to have done the Induction? It's not necessary. You can channel all the time. You can channel for your work, you can channel in your relationships, and you can channel with your children. There's no limitation on when you can channel, or who can witness you channel. The only limitation is that if somebody who has not done the Induction before, wants to learn how to chan¬nel and do the Induction, it must be done by someone who has completed their Level 2, as their energy field is strong enough to enable the Induction.

7.3 HOW TO USE CHANNELING TO CHANGE YOUR LIFE

When channeling is a practice, you have infinite different ways it can be used, and how you can channel to improve your life. *To learn about over 30 techniques & protocols for using your channel you can do the Dira Advanced Channeling Program, which explains how to use channeling to change your life.*

DIRA ADVANCED CHANNELING PROGRAM

7.3.1 CALLING ON DIVINE PROPERTIES

One example is to call of Divine properties. By calling on Divine's properties you can utilize your channel for various purposes in your life. For instance, if you're at the gym and want to lift a certain amount of weight, you can enter into channel and call on Divine strength. This can help you lift more weight and achieve your fitness goals. This approach can be applied to many aspects of your life to enhance your abilities and experiences.

Refer to the following page for Dira's Protocol for Calling on Divine Properties.

DIRA PROTOCOL FOR CALLING ON DIVINE PROPERTIES

Protocol DP 035

1. ENTER INTO CHANNEL
- Use pillar of white light (DP 002).
- Call on Divine using keyword.
- Feel shift in vibration.

2. CALL ON THE DIVINE PROPERTY
- Say "I call on Divine Love to be known to me", it can be any property like Divine Healing, Divine Oneness, Divine Strength etc.
- Amplify the vibration. Say "This vibration amplifies 1000 times on count of 3 - 1,2,3" etc.
- Feel the shift in vibration.

3. MERGING OF VIBRATION INTO PHYSICALITY
- Allow this vibration to fill your body, feel this vibration, and express gratitude: 'I am so grateful for this (the vibration you're calling on)'.
- Say "Merge in my physicality" so that this vibration integrates into your life.

4. CLOSE YOUR CHANNEL
- Touch the heart chakra, expressing gratitude for this possibility by saying 'Thank you'.
- Close channel, asking the energy to recede.

7.4 CONCLUSION

We hope that you enjoyed learning how to channel and we are grateful to have been able to share this possibility with you.

To ensure that you are able to easily integrate channeling into your life, my suggestion is that you find a partner to channel with, and then you can together share this journey of discovering your light. Your partner can be a family member, a friend, a colleague, or someone online. Dira offers a community of people going on this journey with you, so you are not alone in this, and our hope is that this community will continue to grow and the capacity to channel will become the way that people live all over the world.

So, my suggested steps are as follows: You join the group 'New to Channeling', which is on the Dira online platform, if you haven't already. And you share your story and get to know others. You can discuss it with your friends and your family and see if your loved ones would be interested in sharing this journey with you, and identify a channeling partner.

Next, you reflect on how you want to integrate channeling into your life. A morning or evening practice, something you do in the shower, find a way to fit in channeling for five minutes a day, or set up a time once a week where you meet up with your channeling partner to channel together, either in person or online.

You can explore our online platform as there is a significant amount of information on there. If you need extra help with your channeling, like clearing some blocks, reach out on the Dira platform. There are plenty of experienced practitioners that you can book a session with. And if you want to take channeling to the next level, there is the Advanced Channeling Program, as well as the Dira Level Program, and the Magnificent Possibility book.

The Advanced Channeling Program is basically about integrating channeling into your life to be able to change your life. It provides a lot of theoretical information as well as some of the key protocols and exercises that we use at Dira. The Advanced Channeling Program does not however provide a significant amount of time for you to be able to practice those exercises and therefore that is something that you need to do on your own and plan for.

Or you can join the Level Program, which includes the Dira retreats that are the foundation of our offering. These retreats basically enable someone to move through the main seven chakras and allow for the transmutation of their e¬¬ntire energetic system, to be able to be this vessel of Divinity on earth. The Level Program has seven levels. There is the Level 1 which starts at nine days, and the Level 7 takes a year, which you do individually. Visit our website for more information. So, in total, the Level Program takes about three years to complete if you want to do it consecutively. That is also done along with our community, even though you do it in your own time, in your own country. So once again, find a channeling buddy, either through our platform or somebody that you know who might be interested.

The next thing is to familiarize yourself with our online platform. There's so much information that is available to you. And then the next thing is how to deepen your channel. My suggestion is that you look at the Advanced Channeling Program, where you get to learn all of the protocols to be able to integrate channeling into your life and start changing your life for the way that you want to express yourself on this earth.

And lastly, if you haven't gotten a copy yet, the Magnificent Possibility is a book with crucial channeled information that will help you understand the philosophy of life and channeling, the purpose of your existence, and in-depth information on your internal and external toolkit.

Thank you. We look forward to touching base soon.

7.4.1 SUMMARY OF OUR SUGGESTED NEXT STEPS:

- Join the Dira 'New to Channeling' group on the Dira online platform, if you haven't already. Share your story and get to know others.

- Discuss it with your friends and family and see if your loved ones would be interested in sharing this journey with you. Also, identify a channeling partner.

- Reflect on how you want to integrate channeling into your life. A morning or evening practice? Something you do in the shower? Find a way to fit in channeling for 5 minutes a day. Or set up a time once a week where you meet up with your channeling partner to channel together either in person or online.

- Explore our online platform, as there is a significant amount of information on there, and join as a member.

- If you need extra help with your channeling, like clearing some blocks, reach out on the Dira platform. There are plenty of experienced practitioners that you can book a session with.

- If you want to take your channeling to the next level, do the Advanced Channeling Program, start the Dira Level Program, and get a hold of the Magnificent Possibility book.

DIRA ADVANCED CHANNELING PROGRAM

THE MAGNIFICENT POSSIBILITY

DIRA LEVEL PROGRAM

With love,
From all of us at Dira

8. ABOUT THE AUTHOR

Lubna Kharusi is the Founder of Dira and is one of the clearest channelers of Divine Source on the earth today and teaches people how to also become channels of Source.

She was born in the Sultanate of Oman. She is a Chartered Accountant, a trained hypnotherapist, and her Master's thesis was on 'Happiness'. She was the Chief Financial Officer of a multi-billion-dollar government company in Oman. As an unfolding of her spiritual journey, she left her successful career and founded Dira International. Dira's vision is the transmutation of vibration of the world and cosmos, to enable the shift of collective consciousness from separation to Oneness, by using The Dira Method.

The Dira Method was channeled by Lubna, and she has channeled thousands of sessions relating to different forms of transmutation, explanations, and guidance for humanity that enable a shift in the participants, their lives, community, and eventually the world.

In addition, she holds channeled retreats and programs on various subjects for varying purposes. She is the author of 10 books including 'For Humanity'.

In collaboration with IONS, Lubna and Dira channelers were studied and The Dira Method is referenced in the book 'The Science of Channeling' by the world's leading scientific expert on channeling, Helane Wahbeh, as a method for anyone to learn how to channel.

In 2019, in honor and recognition of her work with Dira, she was honored and appointed by the late Sultan Qaboos bin Said Al Said of Oman to the State Council: The Upper House of Oman's Parliament.

8.1 BOOKS BY LUBNA KHARUSI

1. For Humanity, Volume 1
2. I Love you More Than...
3. Fly my Little Butterfly
4. Made of Love
5. I am Perfect
6. Happiness in the Quran
7. Oman: The Journey of Light
8. Dira Basic Channeling - Accessing Divine Consciousness
9. Dira Advanced Channeling – Using Your Channel to Change Your Life
10. Activate Your Abundance - The Keys to Manifestation
11. The Magnificent Possibility - Your Purpose on Earth

www.ingramcontent.com/pod-product-compliance
Lightning Source LLC
Chambersburg PA
CBHW060836170426
43192CB00019BA/2798